MORALITIES

PHILOSOPHICAL STUDIES SERIES

VOLUME 100

The titles published in this series are listed at the end of this volume.

MORALITIES

A Diachronic Evolutionary Approach

by

PAUL ZIFF†

*The University of North Carolina at Chapel Hill,
U.S.A.*

SPRINGER-SCIENCE+BUSINESS MEDIA, B.V.

A C.I.P. Catalogue record for this book is available from the Library of Congress.

ISBN 978-90-481-6537-7   ISBN 978-94-017-0500-4 (eBook)
DOI 10.1007/978-94-017-0500-4

Printed on acid-free paper

per la mia moglie perfetta

Loredana Vanzetto Ziff

Paul Ziff
October 22, 1920-January 9, 2003

ACKNOWLEDGMENTS

Paul was often disdainful of much of the writings on moral theory. He spent almost fifty years doing a systematic study of the major ethicists. This book is the result of his long and thoughtful endeavor. It is written in his own unique style. Since this is Paul's last major philosophical work, I thought that it should be published as written. I was supported in this effort by the wonderful people at Kluwer Press, especially Keith Lehrer and Jaakko Hintikka. I also want to give a special thanks to Ingrid Krabbenbos, Publishing Assistant at Kluwer, for her continued commitment to this project following Paul's death. She has worked diligently to bring this book to press. I want to acknowledge Claire Miller of the Philosophy Department at UNC-Chapel Hill for her support of this project and her willingness to keep the project alive during a period of great stress. Thanks, Claire. Finally, I want to thank Professor Bill E. Lawson for his support and friendship.

Loredana Ziff
November 12, 2003

There are many people to thank for their support in the publishing of Paul Ziff's last major work in Philosophy. I however want to especially thank the three women who made this publication possible. When I came to the project Ingrid Krabbenbos and Claire Miller had completed the more difficult task of organizing the manuscript and getting it ready for publication. Both of these women are to be commended for their efforts and their commitment to Paul's memory. This work was a long term project for Paul and in this regard a special note of thanks must be given to Loredana Ziff whose efforts enabled Paul to finish the manuscript. It is appropriately dedicated to her.

Bill E. Lawson, PhD
Literary Executor of the Estate of Paul Ziff

PREFACE

This essay is the product of years of distaste for, and dissatisfaction with, the efforts of moral philosophers.

It can be tiresome to attend to details, to spell out the obvious, but moral philosophy is such an abysmally difficult subject that faster than a creeping slug is breakneck reckless speed. One simply must content oneself with a slow slimy trail painfully drawn and cautiously constrained.

Generally speaking, philosophy, and, in particular, moral philosophy, is too hard for philosophers.

Even though publishing is spitting in the ocean, and even though my sour sweet spittle will not alter the ocean's salinity, I am somehow inclined to publish this essay.

Acknowledgments:

I began this essay in 1956. During the years, I have discussed many of the topics in this volume with a great many philosophers. I am indebted to all of them, especially those with whom I disagreed and those who disagreed with me. One learns nothing from agreement, whereas disagreement provokes one to look more closely and more carefully at what is at issue: if a philosopher is to profit from discussion, someone must be disagreeable.

Some persons to whom I am indebted are mentioned in footnotes. Others are some of my colleagues at The University of North Carolina, in particular: William Lycan, Michael Resnik and Stanley Munsat. Still others are: Dale Jamieson, Douglas Stalker, Bill Lawson, Bradley Wilson, Frank Sibley, Elliot Cramer, Matthew Ziff,

Rita Nolan and Emily Michael. Undoubtedly there are still others who
have helped me, whose names or aid I cannot recall: *mea culpa*!

I am particularly indebted to Gilbert Harman for having undertaken a
critical examination of this entire essay: his criticisms, comments and
suggestions were extremely helpful. Of course, he is not to be blamed
for what I say or do not say.

> When philosophy paints its gray in gray, then has a shape of
> life grown old. By philosophy's gray in gray it cannot be
> rejuvenated but only understood. The owl of Minerva spreads
> its wings only with the falling of the dusk.
>
> *Hegel*

MORALITIES

1.   The primary thesis of this essay is that, although there are many different and conflicting moralities, both here in America and throughout the world, some of them can be criticized and rejected on rational grounds. There are other moralities that one can personally reject, but they cannot be criticized on rational grounds. The same is true of the various values and priorities that different people have. Some are open to criticism on rational grounds; others are not open to such criticism.

2.   To support this thesis, we shall have to consider a great many different and complex matters: there is no simple and direct way to establish the thesis in question. But even though we shall have to consider many different and complex matters, many different topics, this essay is not divided into chapters, and this for two reasons: first, there is really only one fundamental topic under consideration, namely the primary thesis stated above; secondly, the discussion is designed to be continuous: one question leads to another. Many things stated early on will, of course, depend on what is said later: not everything can be stated simultaneously. Furthermore, one cannot, when dealing with such a difficult topic, avoid what may appear to be digressions: the environs of a question or an answer may have to be explored and clarified, distinctions have to be drawn. Hence patience and careful reading is called for. (My advice to the reader: read through the whole essay without worrying overmuch about details; then read it again making free use of the index.)

3.   It can be tiresome to attend to details, to spell out the obvious, but moral philosophy is such an abysmally difficult subject that faster than a creeping slug is breakneck reckless speed. One simply must content oneself with a slow slippery winding trail painfully drawn and cautiously constrained. The principal sights to be attended to along this trail will be "moral principles", "commitments", "symbolism" and "images".

4.   To begin with we shall have to consider what is being presupposed, and what is being referred to, in speaking of moralities. I shall not, however, try to offer definitions either of "morality" or of "rational": definitions of such familiar terms are not likely to make anything any clearer. Instead, I shall try to make clear what the

relevant parameters and salient features of moralities and rationality are.

5.   Truths are hard to map in moral philosophy: those both credible and of philosophic consequence do not declare themselves to be such. The first truth to be charted is this: appreciably large groups of human beings, groups that endure for an appreciable time as groups, have some sort of moral concerns, some sort of morality.

6.   This is a highly theoretic first truth, for what is in question is not amenable to any direct form of verification. However, given relatively uncontroversial assumptions about the inherent sociality of *Homo Sapiens*, it is unlikely that there be, or that there have been, an appreciably large and appreciably enduring group totally devoid of any sort of morality.

7.   Not only does it appear to be the case that appreciably large and appreciably enduring groups of human beings have some sort of morality, but even proper subgroups of such groups, in the set-theoretic sense of 'proper' of course, often appear to have what appear to be moral concerns. Thus criminal groups consider "stool-pigeons" to be reprehensible. It is sometimes said "There is no honor among thieves". Unfortunately, there is; but honor among thieves is virtue transmuted to vice. Members of "Le Brigate Rosse" adhered to a strict and unrelenting code. Even the CIA and "the Green Berets" pursue various coded paths. Mafiosi types, at least those associated with either the Neapolitan Camorra or the Sicilian Mafia, are required and are expected to respect "the family". The use of the expression "the family", when speaking either of the Sicilian Mafia or of the Neapolitan Camorra, is not a simple minded simile: the family feature of a Mafioso behavioral code, to speak in population-genetic terms, simulates, or possibly even once exemplified, some form of kin selection.

8.   Moralists sometimes speak of moral codes, but what is a code? If one looks to etymology, it is a trunk of a tree, a tablet of wood, covered with wax to write on. But here, first and foremost, it is an abstract system of some sort: a digest of laws; a systematic statement of a body of law; a system of principles or rules.

9.   As far as I know, only human groups have codes, and, *a fortiori*, only human groups have moral codes. (I am not denying the possibility that some other primates have codes of some sort, but, whether or not that is so, does not matter here.)

10.   Insect groups may display highly structured behavioral repertoires, but a behavioral repertoire does not instantiate a behavioral code if the organisms, whose behavior is in question, cannot be aware that their behavior constitutes compliance with or conformance to a code; compliance with or conformance to a code is not possible for organisms that neither have nor can form any conception of themselves. Such organisms cannot be aware that their behavior has a certain character for they are not aware that their behavior is theirs.

11.   Not every organism has a conception of itself: no matter how anthropomorphically minded one may be, no matter how much one may maunder about in misconceived conceptions of organisms, no rational informed being can today be convinced that, say, the cockroach has a clear self-image and, on occasion, may be subject to feelings of remorse, pride, regret, despair, disgust and so forth. I admit to having great respect for the learning capacities of cockroaches, and others of their ilk, but they are not capable of having what appear to be distinctly primate oriented experiences: experiences of guilt, shame, embarrassment, embitterment, hatred, envy, greed, lust, pride and so forth. All such experiences are possible only if one has a conception of one's self: only if, so to speak, one can look into a mirror and say to oneself 'That is me. I see myself in the mirror', or, if one prefers, 'That is my image that I see in the mirror'.

12.   'I', 'me', 'mine', 'myself', 'you', 'yours', 'yourself', 'ours' and so forth serve to express conceptions available only to some of the primates in our world. An entity that has no such conceptions cannot have a morality.

13.   I do not offer this by way of solace, justification or whatever, but the fact of the matter would seem to be that the true blue-bloods of our world, the splendid lobsters, on being captured, caged and turned over to the callous care of a chef, do not lament their fate, do not

experience grief, despair and so forth. Which is certainly not to deny that, if they are not properly treated, they will most certainly experience all sorts of feelings, such as those of danger and alarm, pain and the like. I am also inclined to believe that even the common housefly is capable of, and frequently does, experience feelings of danger and alarm, this being evidenced, in part, by the nonlinear character of its reactions to pursuit.

14.   One could also say that birds, rats and roaches, unlike men, are never fools, which clearly establishes the superiority of *Homo Sapiens*: to be capable of falling from grace into slop is, after all, no small matter.

15.   Do I have a morality? Do I have a moral code? Certainly I have moral concerns: so I have some sort of morality. But the morality that a person conforms to and complies with may be relatively inchoate and unarticulated. Its systematic aspect may be, at best, only possibly implicit. If I have a moral code, it is in remarkably uncodified form.

16.   Moralities and moral codes are to be discerned as one discerns the grammar of an idiolect, or of a dialect, or of a language, which is to say, with considerable difficulty and requiring the exercise of considerable analytic skills. Just as the grammar, the phonology, the syntax and semantics of my own language may be altogether obscure to me, so my own morality, my own moral code, may be something that I can only conjecture about.

17.   The grammar of my language stands to my actual speech as a relatively abstract characterization of a performance stands to the performance. An ability to perform in no way guarantees an ability to characterize. Grammars and moral codes are metatheoretic artifacts.

18.   The sentence 'Thou shalt not covet thy neighbor's wife' serves to express an explicit moral enjoinder; whereas 'It is wrong to covet thy neighbor's wife' serves to express an implicit moral evaluation. Some enjoinders are representable and characterizable as principles, others as precepts, others as maxims and so forth.

19.   The sentence 'Coveting thy neighbor's wife is evil' does not directly serve to express an enjoinder; rather, it serves to express an

explicit moral evaluation. Evaluations, as well as enjoinders, are representable and characterizable in diverse ways. "You ought not to have done that" is an admonishment that serves to convey a negative evaluation, either of what was done or of the doing of what was done; "It was not my fault" is a disclaimer, but it can also serve to convey a negative evaluation.

20. The morality that a person conforms to and complies with is best represented and characterized as a relatively indeterminate collection of moral enjoinders and moral evaluations. If one thinks of this collection on the analogy of a set of theorems, what is then spoken of as the person's moral code is an analogue of an axiomatic base of the set. Any such axiomatic system is likely to be remarkably ill defined and certainly incomplete.

21. The primitive terms of almost anyone's moral conceptual scheme are likely to be vague, amorphous and, almost certainly, necrotic owing to the inevitable moral amaurosis of beings bound to be forever slipping in time's slide.

22. What are the specific characteristics in virtue of which a code may sensibly be classed a moral code?

23. Presumably the code is, at least, concerned with, and pertains to, what is right or wrong, and what ought or ought not be, and with what ought or ought not be done, and with what is good or what is evil, and with what is a vice and what is a virtue, and with what is or is not blameworthy, or what is or is not praiseworthy.

24. To suppose that morality is primarily a matter of heeding enjoinders is to make the mistake of the Kantians. To suppose that morality is primarily a matter of attending to evaluations is to make the mistake of the Aristotelians and Utilitarians.

25. Here, however, one must be aware of, and attend to, the rhetorical factors in any discourse about morality. Thus one must attend to the differences, in familiar discourse, between that which is right, that which is morally right, that which is good, that which is morally good, that which is wrong, that which is bad, that which is morally wrong and that which is evil.

26.   For any act or action, *A*, performing *A* may be right, or it may be good, or it may be morally right or it may be morally good; conversely performing *A* may be wrong, or it may be bad, or it may be morally wrong or it may be evil.

27.   In each case the succeeding terms are, in my dialect anyway, rhetorically stronger than the preceding. If someone finds and promptly returns another person's lost wallet containing a small sum of money, I should be inclined to say that what the person did was right. I would not be inclined to say that what the person did was "morally right" or that it was "morally good": those phrases have a solemn ring to them that sounds out of place when all that is concerned is returning a small sum of money. And if the person kept the wallet for himself then, if there were no complicating factors, I would say that what he did was wrong, but I certainly would not characterize what was done as evil. Money may be the root of much evil, but failing to return a small sum is not, in itself, something evil: it is, perhaps, only wrong.

28.   The example just given to illustrate what I take to be a rhetorical difference between terms is, however, not designed to suggest that there is only a mere rhetorical difference between the terms. Possibly it is an apt example only for some: whether it is an apt example for others depends on their priorities and values. For me, the return of a small sum of money is not a particularly morally important matter.

29.   Which rhetoric one elects may serve to indicate one's priorities and values:

> "Suppose, for instance, that a man pays a particular debt simply from fear of the legal consequences of not doing so, some people would say he had done what was right, and others would deny this: they would say that no moral value attaches to such an act, and that since 'right' is meant to imply moral value, the act cannot be right".[1]

---

[1] W. D. Ross, *The Right And The Good* (Oxford: Clarendon Press, 1946) 2.

30.   Was what was done right? I am inclined to think so. Was it "morally right"? That depends on what morality is in question: for me, the question is moot.

31.   What is right or wrong and what is morally right or wrong are, of course, not identical; and neither are what is good or bad and what is morally good or evil. Not every enjoinder is a moral enjoinder and not every evaluation is a moral evaluation.

32.   "Keep your eye on the ball!" is a technical enjoinder in tennis; not to keep one's eye on the ball is an error in technique: it is wrong not to keep one's eye on the ball; but, with respect to most moralities, it is not morally wrong. A good passing shot wins a point, but, with respect to most moralities, a good passing shot is not of any moral value.

33.   One should not, however, close one's eyes to the fact that there could conceivably be, or have been, some somewhere such that, with respect to their morality, it is or was morally wrong not to keep one's eye on a ball. Or there could conceivably be, or have been, some somewhere such that, with respect to their morality, a good passing shot in tennis is, or was, of moral value.

34.   It need not strain one's powers of conception to conceive of something akin to a Zen sect in which moral values are placed on the development of the physical and psychological abilities requisite for success in such activities as tennis, archery and so forth.

35.   Moralists, unfortunately, often ignore this fact. Thus Prichard claimed that "though we should allow the wanton infliction of pain on ourselves to be foolish, we should not think of describing it as wrong"[2]: possibly he never stopped to think about the reference of "we". For first, if I saw someone inflicting pain on himself, say violently pounding the wall with his fists till they were bloody, I would think that what he was doing was wrong. But, of course, one would want to know why he was doing that. If I attributed his action to insanity, I would still think it wrong, I would still think that he ought

---

[2] H. A. Prichard, *Moral Obligation* (Oxford: Clarendon Press, 1949) 5.

not to be doing that, but I would not deem him to be morally at fault. However, if I attributed his action to frustration and anger, I would be inclined to think he had a defective character. And secondly, in so far as I am prepared to deem his action wrong, and his character defective, I see no reason to suppose that there could not be someone with a morality different from mine who would go further and deem him to be morally at fault: certainly the person is not complying with the enjoinder in the *Revised Version* of the Christian scripture, *The Gospel According to St. Matthew*, to the effect that one shall not be angry.

36.   There is no act or action such that it could not conceivably be, or have been, in compliance, or in conflict, with some conceivable morality or moral code.

37.   One cannot, therefore, simply on the basis of formal properties, determine whether or not a given enjoinder or a given evaluation is a moral enjoinder or a moral evaluation. There is no formal difference between principles of etiquette and principles of morality. (Much the same conclusion can be arrived at from a more traditional approach: "The conclusion we should draw is that moral judgments have no better claim to be categorical imperatives than do statements about matters of etiquette."[3])

38.   "Do not stare at, or attempt to make eye contact with, strange women!": in America, this is, or anyway was, a matter of social proprieties, of etiquette. The obligation is a social obligation; one who fails to conform to the enjoinder is deemed rude. One deemed rude is liable to be subject to social sanctions, possibly significant but, most likely, not violent. In Turkey, one who fails to conform to the enjoinder is, or anyway was, deemed virtually to have sexually assaulted the woman in question: he may be, or have been, subject to violent sanctions.

---

[3] Phillipa Foot, "Morality As A System Of Hypothetical Imperatives" *Philosophical Review*, Vol. 81 (1972) 312.

39.   There is a view, that many subscribe to, according to which the enjoinders of morality are binding in a way that the enjoinders of etiquette are not.

40.   There is a half-truth here: if some class an enjoinder as an enjoinder of "etiquette", in so doing they indicate that they do not feel bound by such an enjoinder in the way they would feel bound if they had classed the enjoinder as an enjoinder of morality.

41.   The fact of the matter is that whether an enjoinder is binding depends on the persons being bound. At a formal dinner, there is a moral obligation not to commit theft, say, not to pocket the host's silverware; there is also a social obligation not to urinate in one's soup publicly and deliberately. There are many who would rather flout the former than the latter, who would, in fact, feel the latter to be the more binding.

42.   One would have doubts about the morality of the person who flouted the obligation not to commit theft.

43.   One would, here in America, quite possibly question the sanity of the person who flouted the social obligation not to urinate in his or her own soup publicly and deliberately; but this, of course, would depend on the particulars of the situation. Such behavior during dinner at, say, the Merion Cricket Club, might be characterized as insane, whereas the same sort of behavior might merely provoke laughter in a New Orleans bar.

44.   Obligations may take on any shape imaginable, and perhaps only the demented manage to escape many or all of them.

45.   There is the obligation to present and comport oneself in a socially acceptable manner in conformance with contextual demands; thus one controls one's mouth and arranges one's face and limbs according to the situation. So, for example, despite the constant provocation, one, unless demented, feels the obligation not to burst into hysterical laughter on listening to the prattle of administrators, deans and chairmen; unless demented, one feels the obligation not to stamp one's feet in response, not to pound on a table and so on. Being greeted on the street, there is the obligation to respond, and, if one is a

civil being, nodded to, one nods back, whether being a civil being is a drag or not.

46. Although a difference between moral obligations and other social obligations is not to be found in a difference in the force or the power of the obligation, a difference can sometimes be found in connection with individual reactions.

47. If I give way to inclination and burst out laughing in the midst of the dean's address to the department, I shall, most likely, later feel some regret for having done so. I shall, most likely, deem myself to have been at fault. Will I feel guilty? Will I have a bad conscience? If I do, then, for me, it was a moral matter. If I do not, then, for me, it was not.

48. The last time I was in such a situation, I did burst out laughing and I did later feel remiss. Did I feel guilty? Did I have a bad conscience? I don't know. I felt remiss. I ought not to have done what I did. Is this 'ought' the 'ought' of moral obligation or merely the 'ought' of social obligation? If I don't know, who could?

49. Whether or not one keeps one's eye on the ball in playing tennis is, for many, not a moral matter; but, for some, it is indirectly a moral matter in at least this sense: it is not immoral to comply with the associated technical enjoinder. That it is not morally wrong to do so is a consequence of some moralities and in accordance with some moral codes.

50. I am inclined to suppose that there are, in fact, groups of persons, sects, such that, for them, such an activity as playing tennis is an immoral activity: for them, it constitutes a concession to frivolity, a failure to appreciate the bitter necessities of life. Would Luther have played tennis?

51. What falls within the domain of the moral depends on the morality in question. The domain of the moral may include anything one may be enjoined to do or not to do: for any X, if one is enjoined to do X, then, possibly, either doing X is morally right or doing X is not morally right or doing X is morally wrong or doing X is not morally wrong.

52.   In contrast, the domain of the aesthetic is more likely to be relatively limited: Leonardo's *Ginevra de' Benci* may be deemed beautiful, Grunewald's *Christ* not, but the number 7 is not likely to be deemed either beautiful or not. Moral matters, however, are not as likely to know such a limitation: the moral may be, and often is, utterly mindless and universal in scope. "Is the number 13 evil?" For me, the question is absurd, but not senseless. If someone says to me "The number 666 is evil: it is the number of the beast", I may think "How pathetic!", but I understand what he says.

53.   The question whether the next cow one sees will remain tangible while being milked is not a question that is apt to occur to anyone in the ordinary course of things. But once the question is posed, one expects a logically adequate physical theory to provide an answer.

54.   The question whether it is or is not morally right or morally wrong to comply with such a technical enjoinder as "Keep your eye on the ball in tennis!" is not a question that is apt to occur to anyone in the ordinary course of things. But once the question is posed, one expects a logically adequate morality to provide an answer.

55.   What is good or bad and what is morally good or evil are, of course, not standardly identical. Fresh vegetables are good but, with respect to a familiar morality, neither morally good nor evil. Not every evaluation need be a moral evaluation.

56.   But a reference, whether primary, or secondary, or tertiary and so on, of every evaluation, just as a reference of every enjoinder, can fall within the domain of the moral.

57.   The domain of the moral may include anything subject to evaluation: for any X, if X is of value, then either X is morally valuable or X is not morally valuable or X is morally disvaluable or X is not morally disvaluable.

58.   To say of a painting that it is a good painting may be to express an aesthetic, not a moral, evaluation of the painting. But such an evaluation can serve indirectly to express a moral condonation of the practice of giving aesthetic attention to paintings. Aesthetic practices,

just as all social practices, can fall within the domain of the moral. Thus it is significant to say "Fresh vegetables are not morally disvaluable", even though this is hardly the sort of remark that one is apt to make in the usual course of a day.

59.   If one were to say, pointing to a knife that an assassin had employed, "That looks to be a very good assassin's knife", in so saying one would be expressing an evaluation of the knife. The explicit reference of the remark is to a knife, yet there is an indirect reference to and, given the realities of rhetoric, an almost unavoidable condonation of the practice of assassination. If one were concerned not to condone the practice, pointing to the knife, one might more sensibly say: "That looks to be a truly evil assassin's knife."

60.   "Can't one simply be commenting on the increase in efficiency that the use of such a knife must have provided?" That could be one's aim, but such a comment could provoke the response: "Is a contribution to efficiency in assassination a value? Is such a contribution to be prized and praised?"

61.   Wouldn't the best assassin's knife be one that precluded the possibility of assassination, perhaps one so fragile that it would guarantee ineffectuality?

62.   "I don't approve of assassination, but can't someone, nonetheless, be an excellent assassin?": what sort of excellence could be in question? One assassin may excel all other assassins in accomplishing his murderous ends: is he, therefore, one who does an excellent job? Again, wouldn't the best assassin be one whose target was never harmed?

63.   "A good knife is a knife that answers to the relevant interests pertaining to a knife. Just so, a good assassin's knife is one that answers to the relevant interests pertaining to an assassin's knife." For some, that will not do. It is no good saying "There is good versus bad and good versus evil and, when I say that that is a good assassin's knife, the relevant contrast is with bad, not evil." Unless one condones assassination, those interests are, for some, not to be countenanced.

64.   When what is in question is evil, there is, for some, no other good but that which contrasts with evil.

65.   Though a person may wish to distance himself from an issue, though he may wish merely to comment on some aspect of the passing scene, the realities of rhetoric are often inescapable.

66.   In the early years of World War II, films were shown in this country displaying the prowess of the German army, the swiftness of the devastation and the "efficiency" of the German blitzkrieg in Poland. I have no way of knowing whether those who showed such films had any specific aim in doing so, but what the showing of such films accomplished was clear enough: it aroused feelings both of admiration and of fear in many of the viewers. It is not unlikely that it strengthened the position of the isolationist forces in America. Was there anything admirable about the blitzkrieg in Poland? Try explaining it to the Polish dead!

67.   It is no discredit to *Homo Sapiens* to give unlimited credit to his capacity for absurdity, aesthetic, moral and intellectual. Even though it may be no more than a covert display of DNA, the diversity of mores and moralities is a paean in praise of the human imagination.

68.   "What do moral codes do?" This, of course, is either a highly elliptical or a foolish question, for, of course, moral codes literally do, and can do, nothing. A code is an abstract system of some sort: abstract systems may mean everything, yet they do nothing.

69.   How does a group that complies with a moral code differ from a group that does not so comply? Or one could equally well, with equal relevance, ask: What difference or differences does it make whether or not a group complies with a moral code?

70.   A specific answer will, no doubt, depend on the specifics of the code, but a more interesting generic characterization is available: one can hardly avoid it, even if one has no appetite for generality.

71.   If a group complies with a moral code, the judgments, evaluations, behavior, attitudes, inclinations and so forth of the group

accordingly exemplify a distinct and specific structuring constitutive of compliance with the code.

72.   The notion of structuring is neither nebulous nor esoteric. A simple way, for example, of structuring the ambulatory behavior of persons at a cocktail party is to place large concrete blocks at strategic positions in the party area: this will give rise to distinct and readily discernible patterns of traffic rippling round and bouncing off the blocks. Structure is a relatively simple topological conception calling for a domain of entities with a set of relations over the domain.

73.   Compliance with either moral or behavioral codes may be instantiated in a modulation of people's attitudes and behavior, but not every apparent modulation is attributable to compliance with a code.

74.   Not compliance with a behavioral code, but my own physiological incapacity prevents me from leaping tall buildings in a single bound. And, if, when at dinner, I would not rise, step atop the table and urinate in an empty plate, it is not because I am constrained by a wish to conform to some code of etiquette; my own disinclination is sufficient to preclude the possibility of such behavior.

75.   Would such outlandish behavior constitute a breach of etiquette? One could as well say that to be mugged is to be treated impolitely. (But this is, perhaps, an intracultural conclusion. Possibly in another culture such behavior would be considered merely an eccentricity.)

76.   How did I acquire a disinclination to urinate atop the table while at dinner? I do not know. Conceivably I did not acquire it: conceivably, though it is not likely, the disinclination is innate. But that is not to say that one could not acquire either an inclination or a disinclination for that which one was innately disposed to have either an inclination or a disinclination for.

77.   The provenance of one's inclinations and disinclinations is not precisely pertinent: the fact of the matter is that I do indeed, as does just about anyone, have various inclinations and disinclinations. It would be nice to know why these things are so, but that could not alter the fact that they are so.

78.   The moral and behavioral codes structuring many of my attitudes and much of my behavior were, by and large, not fashioned by me. Both moral and behavioral codes are sociobiological products; one's compliance with codes is primarily a matter of acculturation, which is not to deny that, for some, and on occasion, and in the passage of time, perhaps with the maturation of neural mechanisms and the evolution of neural structures, there may be elements of choice involved.

79.   In moral philosophy it is essential to understand what is being chosen and where choice lies.

80.   Is it possible not to have any moral concerns, any moral commitments? There are persons in our society who do not seem to have many moral concerns or moral commitments; we may characterize such persons as "amoral", but totally amoral types, apart from some inmates of mental institutions, or ones who should be inmates, are perhaps nonexistent.

81.   Are there some somewhere whose moral concerns and lives are simpler, whose morality admits of easy codification? Possibly one should turn one's attention here to the somewhat demented, to religious fanatics, to cult converts, to the puritanical and the like. For some, there are no problems in conforming to nontrivial, precise and explicit moral principles, principles without qualifications and admitting of no defeasibility conditions. I, and many others, find it impossible to conform to such principles.

82.   Although explicitly formulated moral codes generally have a conspicuous behavioral orientation, one is not warranted in assuming that moral codes are nothing more than specific types of behavioral codes. Such an assumption is often made, either explicitly or implicitly: thus it has been claimed that "... we adopt moral principles when we have reasons to believe that they serve to guide us in right action."[4] To say "we adopt moral principles" is to employ an odd

---

[4] Ruth Barcan Marcus, "Moral Dilemmas And Consistency", (*The Journal Of Philosophy* Vol. LXXVII, No. 3. March 1980) 130.

locution: one adopts policies, procedures, children, stray cats and the like. Moral principles are abstract formulations and expressions of relatively fundamental moral commitments and concerns. One does not, or anyway I do not, "adopt" moral commitments or concerns.

83.   Prichard claimed that:

> "The word 'ought' refers to actions and actions alone. The proper language is never 'So and so ought to be', but 'I ought to do so and so'. Even if we are sometimes moved to say that the world or something in it is not what it ought to be, what we really mean is that God or some human being has not made something what he ought to have made it. And it is merely stating another side of this fact to urge that we can only feel the imperativeness upon us of something which is in our power; for it is actions and actions alone which, directly at least, are in our power."[5]

84.   Prichard ought to have been more careful in his statement, for what he meant, and later said, was that "the 'ought' of obligation is not that of 'ought-to-exist'".[6] There is, however, no reason to accept his view.

85.   No doubt Prichard believed that "it is actions and actions alone which, directly at least, are in our power", but, as any roshi, any Zen master, could have told him, that is not true. Some have the power to control their thoughts, their feelings and emotions. The Zen practice of zazen is concerned with the acquisition of the ability to control every aspect of one's self.[7] To think a thought is to perform an act, not an action. To be calm, to have certain feelings, emotions or desires, is to be a certain way; one enjoined to be calm is not enjoined to perform

---

[5] H. A. Prichard, *Moral Obligation* (Oxford: Clarendon Press, 1949) 4.

[6] *Op. cit.*, 163.

[7] *Cf.* Paul Wienpahl, *The Matter of ZEN: A brief account of Zazen* (New York: New York University Press, 1964).

any action, yet to comply with such an enjoinder is in the power of some.

86.   The commandment, "That shalt not covet thy neighbor's wife", is an element of a Judaic moral code; one is not enjoined not to behave in a certain way, but, rather, one is enjoined not to have a certain desire. Again, in the Christian scripture, *The Gospel According to St. Matthew*, there is an enjoinder to the effect that one is not to be angry without cause. In the *Revised Version* of that text the qualifying phrase, 'without cause', has been deleted, thus one is enjoined simply not to be angry.

87.   There may be a temptation here to suppose that, even though such enjoinders as these do not have an explicit behavioral aspect, they nonetheless have an implicit behavioral aspect.

> "Underneath the abject willow,
> Lover, sulk no more:
> Act from thought should quickly follow.
> What is thinking for?"[8]

88.   But mere thoughts have often been deemed evil, regardless of any behavioral manifestations or consequences; feelings, emotions, desires and thoughts of all kinds have all been subject to prohibitions by various moral codes. Priests have been required to be naked while performing ceremonies with young virgins: erections would then be a visible proof of the character of their thoughts and would be punished by death.

89.   One can make altogether plausible guesses about the *raison d'être* of at least some codes, for example, certain dress codes.

90.   Consider the dress code enforced at many of the tennis and swimming clubs in North Carolina. If one is playing on a court, one is required to wear a tennis shirt. But if one is hitting on a backboard, walking around the grounds, sitting by the swimming pool and so forth, and if one is male, one is not so required. The utility of wearing

---

[8] W. H. Auden

a shirt while playing tennis in the heat is minimal: if there is bright sunlight, the shirt can afford some protection from ultra violet rays; on the other hand, the cooling effect of evaporation is virtually precluded; the clinging soaked shirt can constrain and interfere with one's movements. When my friends and I play on public courts in the August heat, we always remove our shirts and invariably feel the better for it. Clearly, this dress code is of little evident utility: why then does it exist?

91. The answer is obvious enough: the directors and members of clubs who enforce such a dress code are in the grip of an image. The *raison d'être* of the code takes its locus in conformance to the image.

92. I am not suggesting that dress codes are momentous matters. I would not know whether the Horsemen of the Apocalypse are conformists, have crew cuts, wear neat neckties or whatever. But one must, I think, in ethics and in philosophy look closely at small things; in a droplet of water one can sometimes see reflected distant mountains, across which one may have to make one's way.

93. Both birds and men exemplify patterns of behavior in which territorial claims play an active role: "A man's home is his castle", "No trespassing!", "You can't enter without a search warrant!", and so on and on.

94. A bird defending his territory is like a man defending his territory in some respects, but is never like a man defending his territory in certain other respects. The difference is that the territorial defense of the bird is never undertaken as a purely symbolic enterprise.[9] Such symbolic efforts are made only by special primates. Among men, the real significance of a territory may pale into insignificance while its symbolic aspect grows beyond all bounds. Think of the heroic efforts of soldiers in time of war to defend a

---

[9] *Cf.* J. Maynard Smith and G. R. Price, "The logic of animal conflict", *Nature*, London 246: 15-18; J. Maynard Smith, "Evolution and the theory of games", *American Scientist* 64: 41-45.

heavily attacked position, even when the position has no genuine military value. One need only recall the defense of the Alamo.

95.   "Do not think the thought!" is, no doubt, a curious enjoinder. It is nonetheless real. But why not think the thought if the thought does not give rise to an action? Possibly it is the image of one thinking the thought. Consider a young girl, lithe and nubile, a coarse old man looking, leering at her, thinking: form the image. It is, for some, an unpleasant image, one of age'd lust.

96.   There is an enormous bias built into a common perception of man: man is the rational animal. So, it is thought, morality and moral codes must be an expression of this rationality. Moral philosophy seems to have been forever subject to such hubris.

97.   A more plausible perception of men and women is to see them as rational but symbol minded primates, grasping at, driven by and gripped by images. Symbolism and imagery underlie our lives, direct and structure our activities. That symbolism and imagery constitute the real and only basis of morality is what I hope will become apparent in the course of this essay.

98.   Realizing this, and staring into the mirrors of one's own mind, one must make the effort to appreciate and understand this domination. Nothing, however, guarantees that one can escape self-delusion.

99.   Contemplating moralities calls for a vantage point and time provides it: time is the gyre in which human affairs twist and turn. Any and all moralities are subject to diachronic evolution.

100.   The life of an organism of the species *Homo Sapiens*, *H*, is the process or event that begins at the time of conception and ends at the time of death. To speak of *H*'s birth is to speak vaguely of an interface between two periods of time: the first characterized by the nonexistence, the second by the existence, of *H*. To speak of *H*'s death is again to speak vaguely of an interface between two periods of time: the first characterized by the existence, the second by the nonexistence, of *H*. When one dies, one ceases to exist. There is no good reason to think otherwise. (There are no spirits; there are no

supernatural beings. "*En ceste foi je vueil vivre et mourir.*"[10]) The universe is large, but we live on earth: our moralities are therefore bound to be earthbound.

101. Life is not death but living is dying. Dying is not winning or losing, nor is it even like winning or losing, for in dying nothing is being achieved, neither is there any failure of achievement. Dying is a process known only by its product: it is that process that inevitably culminates in death, for if it does not, it is not dying, and any process that inevitably has such a culmination must be the process of dying, which is what living is. Such a question as "Have you been living well lately?" could just as well be expressed by 'Have you been dying well lately?'. We move toward death each day, though, on occasion, the movement may seem retrograde.

102. I think time is splintered, today anyway, for there is no time now that is shared equally by all; I suppose there never was. (For, of course, it is incredibly silly to speak, as some are wont to speak, of "The Age of Reason" or "The Age of Enlightenment" and the like: six pedants do not constitute an age.) There is no such thing as "our time": We each follow separate single spatio-temporal paths that cross and recross not quite but almost at random: transience is the order of the day and nothing stays. If "brevity is the soul of wit", then the world is becoming wittier for its time is growing shorter under a constant rapacious assault. And how can one close one's eyes to the heraldic emblem of the day: a nuclear maniac rampant in a field of bright green folly?

103. The shroud of temporality is difficult to bear. It sets limits to the possibility of putting one's head and world in order; and few priorities fare well when put to a temporal rack. In a short time, there will be no time for answers, but when that happens, I will have no questions.

104. In time, during the process of maturation, human beings acquire moral concerns. Conceptions are formed, come into being:

---

[10] Francois Villon, *Le Testament*.

"The notion that full-fledged moral ideas fell down from heaven is contrary to all the facts with which we are acquainted. If they had done so, it would have been for their own sake; for by us they certainly could not have been perceived, much less applied".[11]

105.   Prior to being conceived, say a child, a number, did not exist. Then is the child or the number therefore any less real, less of an existent entity, after conception?

106.   Conceptions are not immutable: as is everything in time's slide, once formed, they are subject to change, to alteration, to growth and decay. What could be more stable than our conceptions of numbers? Yet our conception of the number 1 has shifted in time: for there was a time when 1 was not the immediate successor of 0 in the series of natural numbers, for there was a time when there was no available conception of 0. (Of course, our conception of numbers has a built in timeless aspect. Once a number is conceived of, it exists (timelessly) in the domain of numbers.)

107.   A conception of morality is not exempt from temporality; neither are conceptions of right and wrong, good and evil, obligation, duty and all the other members of the musty tribe: All shift in the wash and slide of time's waves on our eroding shores.

108.   What the morality is that one acquires in the course of maturation and acculturation can be, for a thinking being, altogether unclear; but, in the course of time, one forms conceptions of commitment, of trust, of giving one's word and of one's word being virtually inviolable; one forms conceptions of the well-being of others and of the well-being of all living things, of the position of others and of what it would be like to be in the position of another. In the course of time these may become fundamental conceptions serving to structure a morality.

---

[11] F. H. Bradley, *Ethical Studies* (Oxford: Clarendon Press, 1935) 190.

109.   Not all conceptions are well-formed: humans, being merely human, have, all too often, misshapen, ill-formed, monstrous conceptual progeny, witness "soul", "pure blood", "ghost" and so on.

110.   Although I am not, in this essay, concerned to provide linguistic analyses of moral terms, it may be of some utility to focus the reader's attention on certain linguistic distinctions here being presupposed.

111.   A distinction to be attended to is that between 'act' and 'action'. To elect to take a shower at 4:00 am is to perform a certain act; to take a shower at 4:00 am is to perform a certain action: there is neither a need to nor any genuine utility in confusing acts and actions.

112.   Acts need not involve activity: one may perform an act by inaction; thus one can perform an act of refusal by not responding to a query, by doing nothing at all. There is not overmuch action in the first act of Hamlet. One who acts strangely may, or may not, perform strange actions.

113.   Actions are physical events: an action at sea, the action of the elbow, the action of a trigger. The right action: for a right handed server in tennis, start the right hand moving before the left; otherwise either the pendulum action of the serve will be lost or the toss will have to be too high. The action of a giant swing on the high bar generally calls for straight arms.

114.   Actions are the same, regardless of the motives, purposes, intentions and so forth of the one who performs the actions. Acts are not.

115.   Writers in ethics often appear to speak indiscriminately of moral principles, moral rules and moral maxims. I suppose there is historical warrant for such usage, and I am not concerned to criticize it here. However, my own terminology is not so conflated.

116.   A rule is, for me, primarily a method of procedure. A rule is appropriate when one is required to act in a robot like manner. For example, I am unable to play chess unless I know the rules of the game; once I do, I can then proceed. Furthermore, a rule provides a method which is applicable in all possible eventualities. Thus if I

know the rule for the Knight's moves, I can always say if any particular Knight's move is allowable or not, in so far as that rule is concerned. Of course, whether a particular move of the Knight is allowable need not depend solely on the rule governing the Knight's moves. Thus there may be an available square to move to, in so far as the rule governing Knight's moves is concerned, but it may not be allowable owing to the rule against uncovering check on one's own King. Nonetheless, as I use the term, a rule is universal with respect to its particular reference class.

117.   A moral principle, for example, "All persons have the right to liberty", is like a rule in that it is also universal with respect to its reference class. It admits of no exceptions whatever. When relevant, it can never be ignored. But a moral principle, unlike a rule, is not a method of procedure. Statements of moral principles express moral commitments; moral principles are important regulative instruments serving to structure a morality.

118.   A maxim, as opposed to a rule, does not either enable or prevent one from proceeding. A maxim of chess is to avoid doubled pawns: whether I adhere to this or not, I would still be able to play the game. Alternatively, a maxim, unlike a rule, is not constitutive of a game. A maxim may be thought of as an avowedly weak form of an inductive generalization. Like any advice, it may sometimes be best to ignore it.

119.   As far as I am concerned, with respect to my own idiolect, there are moral principles and moral maxims but there are no moral rules.

120.   One must, in moral philosophy, contemplate and appreciate the character of conceptual conflicts.

121.   We, each of us, have some sorts of conceptual schemes: we have more or less determinate and more or less systematic groups of conceptions of and about various things. Persons with different conceptual schemes may, owing to the differences between their conceptual schemes, enter into conflict.

122.   'Conflict' is from the Latin 'conflictus', which indicates an act of striking together. Persons with different conceptual schemes are not in conflict simply by virtue of having different conceptual schemes: only when they come together and are at odds, or are about to be at odds, and their being so is attributable to a conceptual difference is one warranted in speaking of an actual conceptual conflict. But, employing an easy and familiar trope, namely metonymy, one may speak of conflicting conceptual schemes when one is in fact concerned with only a potentiality for conflict.

123.   Conceptual conflicts come in all sizes and colors. Attempting to explain to a person that the argument schema:

(A): Q and if P then Q; therefore: P

is invalid, one may find oneself involved in an actual conceptual conflict. A person who reasons in accordance with this schema therewith commits the so-called fallacy of asserting the antecedent. But it would be a mistake to think of this as being bound to be just a simple mistake: different and conflicting conceptions of conditionality, of consequence, of validity and so forth could then be in question.

124.   How is one to think if one is to think that (A) is a tautology, that (A) is a deductive truth? One way to do it would be to conflate deduction and induction. For if if P then Q is true and Q is true, there would then seem to be some confirmation for the claim that P is true. This means that one who so reasoned would have a confused, or anyway, different, conception of deduction.

125.   A more perspicuous example is to be found in the case of one who denies that (B),

(B): $A=A$

is a logical truth on the curious ground that nothing stands in any relation to itself. Thus the person argues that if (B) is a significant statement, the entity referred to by the expression 'A' to the left of the '$=$' sign must be distinct from, and therefore not identical with, the entity referred to by the expression 'A' to the right of the '$=$' sign. Therefore (B) is not a logical truth.

126.   One who so argues is, from my standpoint, conceptually confused. But whether confused or not, the person's conceptual scheme and mine are in conflict. He has, I would say, no clear conception either of relations or of identity. Possibly he would respond that he has different, and preferable, conceptions of each. However, I am not much concerned to consider what such a person might say in response. The plain truth of the matter is that we have an irreconcilable conceptual conflict. The conflict is irreconcilable because there is no way of accommodating both his claim that (B) does not, and my claim that (B) does, serve to express a logical truth. The relevant aspects of our conceptual schemes are radically incongruous.

127.   There is no need to confuse and conflate conceptual and psychological, or, equally, moral and prudential, issues. If I manage to persuade the person to give up what I take to be the silly notion that something cannot be in a relation with itself, he and I may achieve some sort of psychological reconciliation: at any rate, we may cease to quarrel. But the conflict between the conceptual scheme that, after persuasion, he has abandoned and my own conceptual scheme remains.

128.   Whether or not an apparent conceptual conflict admits of a conceptual reconciliation depends on the precise nature and character of the conflict.

129.   It is sometimes possible to find an accommodation for competing conceptual schemes or competing symbolic systems. Thus the apparent conflict between wave and particle theories was resolved when appropriate and accommodating transformations were found. On the other hand, the conceptual conflict between Intuitionistic and Classical theories of logic and mathematics is likely to be irreconcilable.

130.   A conflict between moralities, or between moral codes, stems sometimes, perhaps often but not always, from a primarily conceptual conflict. When that is so, such a conflict rarely, if ever, admits of any conceptual reconciliation.

131.   Conflicts sometimes are, and sometimes are not, reconcilable. To pretend that irreconcilable conflicts do not exist, that conflicts are not an ever present element of moral life, would be an academic exercise in futility.

132.   An unmistakable, but, for many, uncomfortable and disquieting truth to be charted in moral philosophy is this: there are, and have been, different groups having different and conflicting moralities.

133.   There can be no reasonable doubt about this matter; it even admits of a form of proof. I constitute a group of one, my neighbor, another. We have different and conflicting moralities; more specifically, we have different and conflicting conceptions of right, wrong, duty and obligation.

134.   This does not mean, however, that I know what my own moral code is: I do not. I do not even know precisely what my own morality is. I believe that certain things are right, that certain other things are wrong; but there are a great many matters about which I do not know what I believe, and there are a great many matters about which I do not know what to believe.

135.   This form of ignorance is not peculiar to me. Only someone with perfect self-knowledge and a miraculous impossible ability to foresee all future contingencies could have a complete morality. Some, in time, discover and develop and continue to create their own morality.

136.   If I were to view myself in time as a collection of individuals then I, today, have different moral concerns and a different morality, than the person I was many years ago. The moral views I have today conflict with those of that person years ago. Some things that he thought right, I think are wrong. Some things that he was certain were wrong, I am now unsure about. And there are some things that I think are right and others that I think are wrong that he never thought about at all.

137.   Despite my ignorance of precisely what my morality is, I know that my neighbor and I have conflicting moralities. In the killing

season, when he goes into the woods, he sees himself as, and judges himself to be, a sportsman. I loathe the conception of a sportsman as one who, impelled by neither biologic nor economic necessity, kills without even a view to eating what he kills. I judge him an immoral insensitive entity, oblivious to the wrong he does to others, unmindful of his obligations to the unborn and mindlessly unaware of an obligation to make manifest an appreciation of life.

138.   Perhaps the clearest general irreconcilable moral conflict is to be found in connection with the morality of punishment.

139.   Bentham said: "... all punishment is mischief: all punishment in itself is evil."[12] Criminals, however, must be constrained in one way or another: to allow all criminals to be at large would be evil. Most should be incarcerated: not with a view to punishing them, but with a view to protecting the society at large and rehabilitating the criminals in so far as is possible. This is not to deny that even though the purpose of incarceration should not be punishment, it does, in fact, constitute a form of punishment and hence is evil. One may, therefore, be forced to make a choice between the lesser of two evils: allowing a criminal to be at large could be evil; to incarcerate the criminal would be evil. (To minimize the evil of incarceration, Bentham designed a prison, the Panopticon, where the warden would see to it that the prisoners were as happy as possible.[13])

140.   In complete conflict with the view I have just sketched is that of those who insist on retribution: if a person commits a crime, that person deserves to be, and ought to be, punished. Punishment is not something evil but a demand of justice. There is no question of choosing between the lesser of two evils.

---

[12] Jeremy Bentham, *An Introduction to The Principles of Morals and Legislation* (New York: Hafner Publishing Company, 1948) 170.

[13] See Bentham's *Panopticon*, Re-printed and sold by T. Payne, 1791.

141.   As far as I can see, there is no way of reconciling these two views of punishment, these two very different moralities.[14]

142.   I here largely agree with Bentham. All punishment in itself is evil: only the vengeful among us insist on retribution. However, the purposes of incarceration are not only the protection of the society and the rehabilitation of the criminal.

143.   Consider, for example, an infamous Nazi murderer who has escaped to Buenos Aires and who now leads a peaceful family life. He is no longer a threat to the society; neither is there any possibility, or even question, of rehabilitation. He should, nonetheless, be incarcerated. Why? Not because justice demands retribution, but because justice demands and provides affirmation of our moral values: the incarceration of the murderer is a symbolic act in support of our moral values. To incarcerate the murderer would be evil, but not to affirm our moral values would, in such a case, be the greater evil.

144.   It must be emphasized, however, that the incarceration of the murderer has, in this case, only the value of the symbolic act, the act of affirming moral values: there is nothing else to recommend it; nothing else worthwhile is being accomplished.

145.   Conflict is our way of dying and living: it is the human condition. There is no need to await the Apocalypse: white Pestilence, red War, black Famine and pale Death are forever at full gallop on any horizon.

146.   The primary thesis of this essay is that some moralities can be criticized on rational grounds; some, but not all. In the case of the morality that holds that punishment is evil and the morality that holds that it is not, I do not think that either can be criticized on rational grounds.

147.   I and many others, believe that punishment is evil: many many others believe that punishment is not evil. I, personally, vehemently

---

[14] For an attempt at a reconciliation, see John Rawls, "Punishment, from "Two Concepts of Rules" " in *Punishment*, eds. Joel Feinberg and Hyman Gross (Encino, California: Dickenson Publishing Co., 1975) pp. 58-63.

reject that claim, but I do not have any rational grounds on which to criticize that claim. If there were any such grounds, they would have to be grounds for rejecting the retributionist morality. I simply do not know what such grounds can or could be. There is, as far as I can see, nothing irrational about such a morality: I deplore it, but I can do no more than deplore it. Neither, however, is there anything irrational about the morality that holds punishment to be evil.

148.   Some may be inclined to say "It is a truth of logic that either punishment is evil or punishment is not evil", but appealing to logic does not enable us to determine either the truth or the falsity of the statement that punishment is evil. Furthermore, it is far from clear that the statement "Either punishment is evil or punishment is not evil" is a truth of logic. Punishment is evil relative to one morality; it is not evil relative to another morality. It is not a truth of logic that either a trip to Venice, Italy, is a long trip or a trip to Venice, Italy, is not a long trip. Obviously, it depends on where one is: if one is in Verona, Italy, it is not a long trip; if one is in Sydney, Australia, it is a long trip.

149.   Claims about rationality, about what is or is not rational, are claims that should and must be scrutinized in great detail. Rationality or irrationality cannot be established on the basis of moral or even prudential considerations. For the sake both of illustration and clarification, I propose to consider an instance of a claim that a certain preference is not rational, a claim made by two brilliant philosophers, both of whom I consider to be mistaken.

150.   A person in a society can view the world about him from two different perspectives: one personal and the other social. Time and temporality have significantly different roles to play from each point of view.

151.   One can view matters from a social impersonal position, in terms that abstract from, that discount, personal temporal considerations. So viewed, one's society is seen as an indefinitely spatio-temporally extended entity: its life is not to be measured, either in years or centuries or even millennia. Societies come and go, but they have no significant temporal boundaries. One can date the

inception of a state, but hardly that of a society or a culture or a language.[15]

152.   One can also view matters from a personal position in time, in terms of one's own temporality. Any person has a personal private life, a life confined in time, bounded by relatively clearly marked and narrowly restricted finite temporal limits. These limits are sometimes incised in tombstones.

153.   The logical contrast here can be seen in the difference between treading water and treading water for an hour. Treading water is a logically nonterminating action, whereas treading water for an hour is a logically terminating action. Of course, if one is treading water, sooner or later one ceases. But to cease, no matter when, is not to finish. There is nothing to finish. In contrast, if one undertakes to tread water for an hour then, if one quits after an hour, one has finished. So persons may tread water for an hour or so. Societies merely tread water until they drown.

154.   Valuations of goods and benefits, as well as the determination of values and priorities, are likely to be subject to considerable variation and fluctuation when viewed from these two fundamentally different perspectives. Temporal factors are, or may be, amplified under one, while virtually vanishing under the other.

155.   When matters are viewed from a personal perspective, time, and time itself, mere temporal distance, may, for some, alter the valuation of goods and benefits: some would have it that there is something irrational in that. Thus John Rawls has maintained:

"As Sidgwick maintains, rationality implies an impartial concern for all parts of our life. The mere difference of location in time, of something's being earlier or later, is not in itself a rational ground for having more or less regard for it. Of

---

[15] For a discussion of some the difficulties in identifying a language, see Paul Ziff, *Semantic Analysis* 2nd printing (Ithaca, New York: Cornell University Press, 1961) Chapter I. The remark there made, *viz.* "... 401 ad., perhaps the birth century of the English language", is, of course, merely an elaborate trope.

course, a present or near future advantage may be counted more heavily on account of its greater certainty or probability, and we should take into consideration how our situation and capacity for particular enjoyments will change. But none of these things justifies our preferring a lesser present to a greater future good simply because of its nearer temporal position."[16]

156.   Preference based on "the mere difference of location in time" is what Rawls calls "pure time preference". He claims: "In the case of the individual, pure time preference is irrational: it means that he is not viewing all moments as equally parts of one life".[17]

157.   Are Rawls's claims here to be believed? Our time is limited: the best may have already been and the worst may be yet to come. It would not be surprising. Given the maturation and inevitable consequent decay of physiological and neurophysiological mechanisms, is a pure time preference nonetheless irrational?

158.   If one is to object to Rawls's claims, one must, of course, understand them. To that end, it helps to separate what appear to be the two primary claims being made.

159.   First, according to Sidgwick and Rawls, "rationality implies an impartial concern for all parts of our life", and, according to Rawls, not to view "all moments as equally parts of one life" is irrational: that is the first claim being made: is it to be believed?

160.   When is one supposed to be so concerned and when is one to have such a view? I had no such concern at the age of five. Perhaps I was not rational at the age of five. At what age, if any, did I achieve rationality? At fifteen I gave no thought to and had no concern for my life at five. Had I thought to look to my life at ninety, I would not have known where to stare: I still would not. At seventy five, I am not genuinely concerned with what was my life at five. How can one treat all parts of one's life as of equal value?

---

[16] *A Theory of Justice* (Cambridge, Mass.: Harvard University Press, 1971) 93-94.
[17] *Op. cit.*, 95.

161.   There is no reason to suppose that questions of impartiality, of fairness and the like, have any clear sense when the domain of application is over such peculiar entities as the moments of one's life. Impartiality has to do with being fair (a conception that we shall have look at later), with fairness and a lack of bias. If I am to have an impartial concern for all parts of my life then, does that mean that I must have the same concern for all parts? But that is logically impossible: it is logically impossible to have the same sort of concern for all parts of one's life.

162.   One can be concerned with the past as a guide to present or future action: one cannot be concerned with either the present or the future as a guide to past action. One can be concerned with the present or the future in that one is concerned to bring about certain present or future states of affairs: one cannot be so concerned with the past, one cannot be concerned to bring about certain past states of affairs. Or, of course and in a sense, one can, for what I do now will, tomorrow, be what I did yesterday; so one is constantly arranging the past. But the difference remains: one can plan for the future, not for the past. One cannot prevent the mistakes of the past, but one can attempt to prevent their recurrence.

163.   The present is the leading edge of the future, the receding edge of the past: it is the interface between past and future. Looked at closely, one can do nothing about the present, for it takes time to act. But one can genuinely do something about the future. So perhaps the Sidgwick-Rawls claim is to be construed to the effect that it is irrational not to have an impartial concern for all the future moments of one's life.

164.   No rational being is really apt to treat the moments of his life equally. At the age of forty, I might be prepared to sacrifice some of my temporally proximate hours for the sake of later hours. Thus I might accede to my dentist's demand that old fillings be replaced: I might submit myself to his tortures. At the age of ninety, I am less likely to make such a sacrifice.

165.   We, each of us, have some sort of life expectancy. At the moment that this is being written, which moment I herewith designate

M, I expect to live N more years; let E, for end of course, be the moment $M+N$. Now consider a graph of a function of *Concern over Time* for my life from now until its expected end. In particular, let L, for life remaining, be the line from M to E, and consider the slope of L.

166.   According to Sidgwick and Rawls, rationality requires that L be a flat horizontal; otherwise one is irrational. In truth, a rational curve is much more difficult to characterize, but certain aspects are perfectly clear.

167.   I cannot conceive of a rational being for whom L would be a flat horizontal. I know of no apt term to characterize the curvature of L, but, for a rational being, despite meanderings, L asymptotically approaches zero.

168.   That L is bound to meander is an inescapable fact of life. Is it irrational to go to an ocean beach even if the drive to the ocean is a chore? So one sacrifices the moments of driving for the moments at the shore. Of course a rational being may try to maximize the value of those moments, but there is little that can be done if one is forced to creep along in a traffic jam, breathing in the noxious fumes of the surrounding cars and keeping an attentive eye open for demented drivers. Or consider a rain delay when one is playing in the finals of a tennis tournament: one finds ways to pass the time. One attempts to be as unconcerned as possible; there is then no rational alternative.

169.   That L asymptotically approaches zero can be seen in this: a rational being is more likely to be more concerned with the day before the expected day of his death than with the expected day of his death, for, ignoring other factors, on the day before the expected day of his death, he expects there still to be a future, albeit a brief future, to be faced.

170.   It will help to look at the Sidgwick-Rawls claim that "rationality implies an impartial concern for all parts of our life" from a different perspective. One can think of oneself as constituted by a series of persons in time: thus I am the set of persons $\{P\}$ whose members are the persons $P1$, $P2$, ..., Pm, ..., Pe, where subscripts 1, 2, ..., m, ..., e are successive temporal indices. Let 1 be the index of my

birth, e of my death and m of the present moment. Then the Sidgwick-Rawls claim is that it is irrational for me not to have an impartial concern for all members of the set $\{P\}$.

171.   When one attends to the realities of life, to the contingencies of daily existence, one can see at once, however, that there is no way in which $Pm+1$, $Pm+2$, ..., Pe can receive equal treatment: some must be sacrificed for others. If one sits through a dean's boring discourse for the sake of future harmonious relations with the dean, has one been irrational? Presumably not, but, if not, the Sidgwick-Rawls claim must either be rejected or reconstructed. An obvious reconstruction is this: it is irrational not to be concerned with the greatest good of the greatest number of the members of the set $\{P\}$. So construed, the claim is evidently a contentious claim to the effect that it is irrational not to adopt Bentham's famous Principle of Utility with respect to the moments of one's life.

172.   The second claim being made is this: The mere difference of location in time, of something's being earlier or later, is not in itself a rational ground for having more or less regard for it.[18] Thus we are not justified in preferring a lesser present to a greater future good simply because of its nearer temporal position.

173.   Let G be a good, I a temporal interval, and $<$, $=$, and $>$ indicate less than, equal to and greater than in value, respectively, and let $+$ indicate what I trust you think it would: then the claim being made is that, given that $Gi<Gj$ (where superscripted indices are merely atemporal numerical identifiers such that $i<>j$, i.e., that i is not equal to j), it would be irrational to prefer $Gi+Ii$ to $Gj+Ij$ (where $Ii<Ij$). This claim would, it seems, be true if it were the case that, for all values of I, $Gi+Ii$ and $Gj+Ij$ are inevitably bound to be constant in relative value.

174.   The question then is: can mere temporal proximity alter value? For if the temporal proximity of a lesser present good can serve to increase its value, and if the temporal remoteness of a greater future

---

[18] *Ibid.*

good can serve to decrease its value, then the lesser present good may prove to be of greater value than the greater future good.

175.   A *locus classicus* of the claim that "propinquity", temporal proximity, can alter value is to be found in Chapter IV of Bentham's *Introduction*:

> "To a person considered *by himself*, the value of a pleasure or pain considered *by itself*, will be greater or less, according to the four following circumstances: 1. Its *intensity*. 2. Its *duration*. 3. Its *certainty* or *uncertainty*. 4. Its *propinquity* or *remoteness*".[19]

176.   Bentham adds in a footnote that "These circumstances have since been denominated *elements* or *dimensions* of *value* in a pleasure or a pain."[20] It is important to notice that Bentham is not here concerned to list what some might call the "qualities" or "properties" of pleasures or pains: he is concerned with factors that serve to determine the value of a pleasure or pain. An intensity may indeed be a quality of a pleasure, but Bentham is here concerned with intensity, not because it is such a quality, but because it is an important factor serving to determine the value of a pleasure.

177.   Despite the fact that Bentham made it altogether clear that he was concerned with factors that serve to determine the value of a pleasure, Sidgwick, in a discussion of hedonism, writes:

> "Bentham gives four qualities of any pleasure or pain (taken singly) as important for purposes of Hedonistic calculation: (1) Intensity, (2) Duration, (3) Certainty, (4) Proximity. If we assume (as above argued) [see below] that Intensity must be commensurable with Duration, the influence of the other qualities on the comparative values of pleasures and pains is not difficult to determine: for we are accustomed to estimate

---

[19] Jeremy Bentham, *An Introduction to The Principles of Morals and Legislation* (New York: Hafner Publishing Company, 1948) 29.

[20] *Ibid*.

the value of chances numerically, and by this method we can tell exactly (in so far as the degree of uncertainty can be exactly determined) how much the doubtfulness of a pleasure detracts from its value; and *proximity* is a property which it is reasonable to disregard except insofar as it is a particular case of certainty. For my feelings a year hence should be just as important to me as my feelings next minute, if only I could make an equally sure forecast of them. Indeed this equal and impartial concern for all parts of one's conscious life is perhaps the most prominent element in the common notion of *the rational* - as opposed to the merely *impulsive* - pursuit of pleasure".[21]

178.   (Although I am not concerned to discuss historical matters here, I must say that I find it simply ludicrous to think of Bentham as a hedonist, let alone a psychological hedonist. As anyone who has read Bentham's collected works, and anyone who reads him from a reasonable historical perspective, should know, by "a pleasure" Bentham simply meant anything that induced, or tended to induce, a person to perform an act or action. To document this claim would, however, require a long scholarly excursus that would here constitute an unwarranted digression.)

179.   The "above" argument that Sidgwick is referring to is an argument to the effect that the intensity of a pleasure can be balanced against its duration:

> "... for if one pleasure, finite in duration be intensively greater than another in some finite degree, the latter may be increased extensively until it just balances the former in amount".[22]

180.   There are so many errors here that it may be difficult to appreciate which are important and which are not. First, as I have already indicated, not qualities or properties of pleasure but, rather,

---

[21] *Methods of Ethics*, 2nd edition, 111-112.
[22] *Ibid.*

factors which serve to determine the value of pleasures are in question. Secondly, it is not true that the intensity of one pleasure can be "balanced against" the duration of another. The pleasure of a sexual orgasm is likely to be intense, the pleasure of eating chocolate ice cream is not likely to be as intense. There is no way in which the pleasure of the latter "may be increased extensively until it just balances the former in amount". Extensively increasing the pleasure of eating chocolate ice cream is likely to result in nothing but nausea. But thirdly, and importantly, Sidgwick grants that the "doubtfulness of a pleasure" may detract from its value, yet he simply fails to discuss whether or not the propinquity, the temporal proximity, of a pleasure may enhance its value. He does say that this factor should be disregarded because one should have "equal and impartial concern for all parts of one's conscious life".

181.   Sufficient reasons have already been adduced above for rejecting the unreconstructed claim that one should have "equal and impartial concern for all parts of one's conscious life", but even if it were accepted, it would not suffice to establish that propinquity cannot enhance the value of a pleasure.

182.   Suppose that at twenty I am offered a choice of two loans: I may have either a small Cezanne sketch immediately to keep for one month or, in five years, one of Cezanne's great oils, again to keep for one month. Does nothing warrant opting for the immediate loan of the lesser work? What if the temporal difference were ten, or even twenty years: does nothing warrant electing not to delay for twenty years? What is in question is a matter of values: can the lesser good, solely in virtue of its temporal proximity, ever yield the greater value?

183.   Suppose I suppose, as I do indeed suppose, that my interest in Cezanne in five years will be the same as my interest now: thus I fully expect to live another five years. Furthermore, I suppose that my capacity and ability to derive aesthetic value from the works of Cezanne will remain unimpaired and unaltered. Thus I can imagine myself, five years hence, viewing the great Cezanne oil with great delight. Then, if I opt for the immediate loan of the lesser work, according to Rawls, I am being irrational, and according to Sidgwick, I

am abandoning the rational, as opposed to "the merely *impulsive* - pursuit of pleasure".

184.   This claim must, if it is to be understood, be scrutinized closely. Again, where G is a good, I a temporal interval, and $<$, $=$, and $>$ indicate less than, equal to and greater than in value, respectively, and $+$ again indicates what I trust you think it would, then, for $i<>j$ and where again $Ii<Ij$, if Rawls and Sidgwick are right, it is not possible, given that $Gi<Gj$, that $(Gi+Ii)>(Gj+Ij)$; thus it is necessary, given that $Gi<Gj$, that $(Gi+Ii)<(Gj+Ij)$. This means that the mere passage of time must be value neutral.

185.   What warrants the claim that the mere passage of time must be value neutral?

186.   The facts of the matter in our real and only world are clear enough: to acquire a temporally remote benefit, or to achieve a temporally remote good, a passage of time is required: that passage will inevitably have a character and its character may be such as to render it valuable, or disvaluable, or neutral with respect to value. Thus, for example, on occasion, such a passage may be a matter of anxiously waiting: in estimating the value of the temporally remote, it would be irrational to discount the possible disvalue of such waiting. (Whether Sidgwick was prepared to discount the possible disvalue of a passage of time is unclear: he was prepared to consider "how much the doubtfulness of a pleasure detracts from its value", but how can "doubtfulness" detract from the value of a pleasure save by rendering the passage of time, that time requisite for the experience of the pleasure, disvaluable, say by making that period of time a period of anxiety?)

187.   For $i<>j$ and where again $Ii<Ij$, it is in fact altogether possible that even if $Gi<Gj$, that $(Gi+Ii)>(Gj+Ij)$. It is also possible, given that $Gi<Gj$, that $(Gi+Ii)<(Gj+Ij)$ or that $(Gi+Ii)=(Gj+Ij)$. Furthermore, it is also possible that $(Gi+Ii)<(Gi+Ij)$ or that $(Gi+Ii)=(Gi+Ij)$ or that $(Gi+Ii)>(Gi+Ij)$.

188.   What I am pointing to here are simple facts of human experience. Some things one wants now, immediately: tomorrow's drink does not slake today's thirst. Some things one wants over and

done with now: tomorrow's tribulations may be worsened by today's anxieties. Some things want waiting for, for anticipation can heighten the value, say, of an amorous encounter after a long walk through green gardens. Some things, all too many, sour in time: the reward, too long awaited, may prove to be no reward at all.

189.   This is not to deny that there are cases in which $(Gi+Ii)=(Gi+Ij)$. But this is only to say that, on occasion, the temporal location of goods, benefits and so forth may be value neutral. Thus, it may be a matter of indifference to me whether I receive delivery of a book this week or the next: I may have no time to read it this month. But if the claim that "mere" temporal proximity or remoteness cannot alter value is construed along these lines, it is a virtual tautology: when a passage of time is value neutral, it cannot alter value.

190.   However, it must be made clear, and understood, that none of the above considerations have any real bearing on the Rawlsian claim that the "mere" passage of time must be value neutral. For what is in question is, not a passage of time having a specific character, in virtue of which it may be evaluated, but, rather, a mere passage of time considered in abstraction from any nontemporal character whatever. Thus, for $i<>j$ and where again $Ii<Ij$, if $Gi<Gj$, then rightly understood, the Rawlsian claim is that, for any intervals considered in abstraction from all nontemporal characteristics, it would be irrational to prefer $Gi+Ii$ to $Gj+Ij$. But what makes such a preference irrational?

191.   Suppose one again conceives of oneself as a series of persons through time: thus, again, I am the set $\{P\}$ whose members are $P1$, $P2$, ..., Pm, ..., Pe. (One may note that temporal position 1 is known to me, temporal position e is not.) If I then opt for $Gi+Ii$ over $Gj+Ij$, I am, in effect, then giving preferential treatment to Pi over Pj. But what if I opt for $Gj+Ij$? Then, in effect, I am then giving preferential treatment to Pj over Pi. In the first case, Pi acquires Gi, in the second case, Pj acquires Gj. Either way, I am committed to, and cannot possibly avoid, an inegalitarian treatment of Pi and Pj.

192.   On the Rawlsian view, given that $Gi<Gj$, it would be irrational to opt for $Gi+Ii$ over $Gj+Ij$. This means that rationality is supposed to require one to give preferential treatment to Pj. Why would it be

irrational to give preferential treatment to Pi? The obvious answer is this: it is irrational not to be concerned with the greatest good of the greatest number of the members of the set $\{P\}$; given that $Gi<Gj$, the greatest good of the greatest number is accomplished by giving preferential treatment to Pj. So, again, the claim is evidently a claim to the effect that it is irrational not to adopt Bentham's famous Principle of Utility with respect to the moments of one's life. From this perspective, the first and second claims are one and the same.

193.   Is it irrational not to be concerned with the greatest good of the greatest number of the moments of one's life? Suppose one does conceive of oneself as a series of persons through time: thus again one is the set of persons $\{P\}$ whose members are the persons $P1$, $P2$, ..., Pm, ..., Pe, where subscripts 1, 2, ..., m, ..., e are successive temporal indices. Again, let 1 be the index of one's birth, e of one's death and m of the present moment. Is it irrational for a person not to be concerned with the greatest good of the greatest number of the members of this set?

194.   There is nothing one can now do about $P1$, $P2$, ..., $Pm-1$; neither is there anything one can do about Pe (except perhaps to commit suicide in a cheerful moment). So all one can sensibly be concerned with is the set whose members are Pm, ..., $Pm+n$, where, of course, the value of $\underline{n}$ is unknown to one. Is it irrational not to be concerned with the greatest good of Pm, ..., $Pm+n$?

195.   Let j be such that $m<j<n$ and consider the set, $\{J\}$, whose members are Pj, $Pj+1$, ..., Pn. This set is a proper subset of the set $\{P\}$. It is very clear that people engage in all sorts of extremely perilous and imprudent activities that suggest that they are not greatly concerned about the members of $\{J\}$. But, if so, can one maintain that they are truly concerned with the greatest good of Pm, ..., $Pm+n$?

196.   Think of people who climb or attempt to climb Mt. Everest. Just think of sky diving, hang gliding, driving racing cars and so on. Every so often these activities result either in injury or in the death of the person, thus $Pj+i$ may prove to be identical with Pe. Should one say that such persons are irrational? Is it irrational to attempt to climb Everest while knowing what the risks are?

197.   I think that the best that one can say about those who undertake such risks is that there is no reason to think that they are truly concerned with the greatest good of Pm, ..., $Pm+n$. Such persons are, perhaps, extremely imprudent: being extremely imprudent, however, is not equivalent to and does not entail being irrational. Some people choose to live at risk, to take chances. Think of a rock climber climbing a surface that many others have climbed before. If he or she succeeds, the reward for doing so is apt to be purely and only symbolic; failure may have not only symbolic but practical consequences, broken limbs or even death.

198.   There is, however, another claim, implicit in the preceding discussion, that must be considered. A fundamental premise of the preceding arguments was that, given that the nontemporal character of temporal intervals is to be discounted, then necessarily $(Gi+Ii)=(Gi+Ij)$. The "mere" passage of time, time considered in abstraction from any nontemporal character, cannot alter the value of anything. Indeed, this would appear to be Rawls's fundamental claim in the initially cited passage under consideration. But time, even in abstraction from all nontemporal considerations, still has a character.

199.   What is a "mere difference of location in time"? If what were in question were simply a matter of dates, where dates are merely assigned numerals in some symbolic system, then there would be little to discuss, in so far as moral matters are concerned. It need not matter greatly, in the abstract, how one dates the periods of one's life. But neither Rawls nor Sidgwick can be construed as concerned with questions of designation. So construed, the question of pure time preference is, in so far as morality is concerned, of minimal significance.

200.   Which is not to say that it is of no significance whatever: the character of the designations we employ can be of considerable significance. It would be vastly more reasonable to designate this year, say, the fifteen billion six thousand five hundred twenty third, or whatever the best cosmological theory indicates, rather than the absurd one thousand nine hundred ninety sixth. Possibly the use of such a

designative term would serve to encourage a more rational attitude about life on earth.

201.   What is a "mere difference of location in time"? The answer depends on one's conception of time. What determines direction in time? I suppose that entropic degradation is the primary factor. According to the second law of thermodynamics, randomness increases in this world, and there is, for us, no other; in time we grow old, we move toward death; in time we become pluralized, we become our remains: the plight of Humpty Dumpty awaits us all. There are, of course, systems in which entropy decreases, but these are not closed systems: pockets of decreasing entropy are merely parasites of the universe. Living organisms do not contravene the second law.

202.   Unlike societies, human beings, persons, have relatively determinate finite temporal limits. Caught in time's slide, inevitably, we grow old, we age, we suffer entropic degradation. As the metaphysically minded Humpty Dumpty might have remarked: Later is worse.

203.   Consider the claim, made by a firm follower of Humpty Dumpty, that, discounting all nontemporal factors, necessarily $(Gi+Ii)>(Gi+Ij)$, where $Ii<Ij$. Rawls's implicit claim is that, discounting all nontemporal factors, necessarily $(Gi+Ii)=(Gi+Ij)$. Evidently, either one or both are in error. There are, of course, another alternatives that could be considered: for example, discounting all nontemporal factors, necessarily $(Gi+Ii)<(Gi+Ij)$: "Grow old along with me! The best is yet to be," *Rabbi Ben Ezra*, Robert Browning's fine line of Victorian nonsense here comes to mind. However, W. B. Yeats's *Why Should Not Old Men Be Mad?* has a more plausible air.

204.   Rawls does say: "... we should take into consideration how our situation and capacity for particular enjoyments will change." That, however, is merely a nod in recognition of the nontemporal characters of temporal intervals. But that we grow old, that we age, that we suffer entropic degradation are facts about being beings in time.

205.   Is it true that, discounting nontemporal matters, if $Gi<Gj$ then, necessarily, $(Gi+Ii)<(Gj+Ij)$? Again, consider the immediate loan of a small Cezanne sketch as against a later loan of a great Cezanne oil. In

such a case it seems clear that $Gi<Gj$. Does it then follow that $(Gi+Ii)<(Gj+Ij)$? Not for a follower of Humpty Dumpty who prizes the immediacy of matters: not for one, perhaps such as Bentham, who is committed to the principle that propinquity enhances value.

206.   Is it, or would it be, irrational to be committed to the principle that, discounting nonspatio-temporal considerations, and letting 'I' and its superscripted indices now represent not merely temporal but spatio-temporal intervals relative to one's own spatio-temporal position, if $Gi=Gj$ then $(Gi+Ii)>(Gj+Ij)$? One could hardly fault such a commitment on the grounds of consequences: from a biological standpoint, such a commitment would seem to be conducive to survival. And certainly many would seem to be committed to some such principle: many of us feel a greater obligation to aid and abet our neighbors than persons more spatio-temporally remote.

207.   Furthermore, letting B be something bad or evil, many would certainly hold that $(B+Ii)>(B+Ij)$, which is simply a cumbersome way of saying that, all other factors being discounted, it is better to suffer something bad or evil later rather than sooner, next year rather than next week.

208.   Or, to view the matter in still another way, suppose one were "under a veil of ignorance" and one was obliged to make a determination for an unknown other. The other is to receive an unknown good or benefit either next week or next year: wouldn't one allocate the good or benefit next week rather than next year? And suppose the other is to suffer an unknown evil or something bad: is there no rational ground for allocating the bad or evil to the other next year rather than next week? Even "under a veil of ignorance" one can hardly be supposed to be oblivious to the fact that, no matter what, the other has only a brief finite life span. After all, the person may be dead before the year is over. And anyway, if one does opt for allocating the good next week and the bad next year, there is not the slightest reason to suppose that such a determination is in anyway irrational.

209.   Even if one were committed to a principle of utility with respect to the moments of one's life, if one were also committed to a principle of propinquity, and possibly committed to a realistic and

pragmatically oriented unprincipled adjudication between conflicting principles, one could readily hold that, all nontemporal factors being discounted, if $Gi=Gj$ then $(Gi+Ii)>(Gj+Ij)$. In consequence, with an appropriate adjustment of values, it should be possible that $Gi<Gj$ yet $(Gi+Ii)>(Gj+Ij)$. There is, as far as I can see, no reason whatsoever to suppose that a "pure time preference" is irrational. On the contrary.

210.   And what does this imply about later generations? Nothing at all: for what has been in question is an individual's pure time preference with respect to the moments of his own life. If one were to consider a pure time preference from a group or social, rather than an individual, viewpoint then all the previous considerations would undergo a sea-change.

211.   If one views the world as a four dimensional space-time manifold, a benefit that is in the distant future of one individual may then be seen to be in the immediate future of another. From such a perspective, time preferences of the individuals constituting the group may be canceled out: a temporally remote benefit for one may be an immediate benefit for another. Indeed, in so far as the group is conceived of as indefinitely spatio-temporally extended, from the group standpoint, there can be no such thing as a temporally proximate or a temporally remote good. Hence such a group cannot have a time preference: thus there is no need to worry about its rationality.

212.   If one were to restrict one's attention to political and social goods and benefits, then perhaps one could argue that since, from the standpoint of the indefinitely spatio-temporally extended society, there can be no temporally proximate or remote goods or benefits, a person, as a member of the society, cannot rationally evaluate social or political goods or benefits from a personal temporal, rather than a social atemporal, perspective. Hence, for the person, as a social and political being, it would be irrational to have a pure time preference with respect to social or political goods or benefits.

213.   But as against this, one cannot overlook the fact that persons lead private as well as social and political lives. There is nothing irrational in taking both private and public needs into one's personal considerations: it is not a requirement of rationality that one have one's

eyes fixed only on others or on later generations. And anyway, will there be later generations? Our world's nuclear maniacs may still be asleep, but they are stirring restlessly: they will awaken before long.

214.   An appreciation of the rationality of appeals to temporal factors is of the utmost importance in a philosophic appreciation of a morality.

215.   According to the analysis just presented, the arguments of Rawls and Sidgwick relied essentially on an appeal to Bentham's famous Principle of Utility. It is therefore necessary to examine and consider that principle, and in some detail. Furthermore, they also relied on considerations of impartiality, and so on a conception of fairness; hence that conception must be examined. The absolutely fundamental point that I am trying to make clear is that the rationality or irrationality of an act or action or preference or value cannot be established on the basis of moral or prudential considerations. (How such matters can be established will be illustrated later in this essay.)

216.   Jeremy Bentham was an admirable person, a secular saint. But saints do not contact this world, and saints have little understanding of merely human difficulties. So one must attend to, and rid oneself of, all futile appeals to the famous principle of utilitarianism:

> "By the principle[1] of utility is meant that principle which approves or disapproves of every action whatsoever, according to the tendency which it appears to have to augment or diminish the happiness of the party whose interest is in question: or, what is the same thing in other words, to promote or oppose that happiness. I say of every action whatsoever; and therefore not only of every action of a private individual, but of every measure of government."[23]

---

[23] Jeremy Bentham, *An Introduction to The Principles of Morals and Legislation* (New York: Hafner Publishing Company, 1948) 2.

217.   In the footnote to the word "principle", Bentham noted that the word "is applied to any thing which is conceived to serve as a foundation or beginning to any series of operations".[24]

218.   Moral principles, as I conceive of them, are abstract formulations and expressions of fundamental moral commitments. They are concerned with matters of fundamental importance to the persons whose principles they are. The principle of utility, as Bentham presented it, has the appearance of being such a principle. (R. M. Hare has said:

> "The moral judgment 'You ought not to smoke in this compartment' has to be made with some general moral principle in mind, and its purpose must be either to invoke that general principle or to point to an instance of its application. The principle might be 'One ought never to smoke in compartments in which there are young children' or 'One ought never to smoke in compartments in which there is a "No Smoking" notice'."

I find it barely conceivable that not smoking in a compartment with young children present be a matter of moral concern requiring a fundamental moral commitment. What is in question here is a radical difference either in terminology or in morality.[25])

219.   Bentham's principle can be construed as being two distinct principles: one concerning individuals, the other concerning the society at large. Indeed, one must attend to alternative construals, for the problems posed differ radically depending on whether one focuses on individuals or on the society at large.

220.   Construed in reference to an individual, the principle of utility says that an act or action is to be judged right "according to the tendency which it appears to have to augment or diminish the happiness of the party whose interest is in question."

---

24 *Ibid.*

25 R. M. Hare, *The Language Of Morals* (Oxford: Clarendon Press, 1961) 176.

221.   For some, the first fundamental question of ethics is: "Should anyone do what is right when doing so is not to his advantage and if so why?"[26] That is not a serious question for me. If I deem it morally right to perform a certain act or action, A, and morally wrong to refrain from performing A, perhaps it could, nonetheless, be to my disadvantage to perform A. Say I would lose goods, or a position, or fame or whatever one can think of: that is simply irrelevant. If I deem it morally right to perform A, and also morally wrong not to perform A, then I am morally committed to performing A: being so committed, I simply must perform, or do my best to perform, A. I have no choice: as Luther said, "Ich kann nicht anders!" - I cannot do otherwise. (Why this is so will, I hope, become evident by the end of this essay.) Let it be clear, however, that the conjunction, and the associated rhetoric, are here significant: if it is morally right to perform A but it is not morally wrong not to perform A then, given that performing A is to my disadvantage, I may have sufficient reason not to perform A. Thus, for example, one is not morally at fault for refraining from an act of supererogation.

222.   Neither can the question be a serious question for Bentham:

> "Of an action that is conformable to the principle of utility one may always say either that it is one that ought to be done or at least that it is not one that ought not to be done. One may say also, that it is right that it should be done; at least that it is not wrong that it should be done: that it is a right action; at least that it is not a wrong action".[27]

223.   (Bentham continued: "When thus interpreted, the words *ought*, and *right* and *wrong*, and others of that stamp, have a meaning: when otherwise, they have none." Moore, and others, have taken Bentham to be here stating a definition of 'right'. Most likely Moore never actually read Bentham's footnoted edition of *The Introduction*, else how could

---

[26] Kurt Baier, *The Moral Point of View* (Ithaca, New York: Cornell University Press, 1958) 3.
[27] *Op. Cit.*, 4.

he have overlooked the elaborate notes on 224-225? Right is one "of those fictitious entities, of which the import can by no other means be illustrated than by showing the relation which they bear to real ones"(225).)

224.   If by "advantage" one understands that which augments the happiness of the party in question, then, given the principle of utility cited above, it is not possible that the action be right and yet not be to the person's advantage.

225.   Kurt Baier claims:

> "We ordinarily use the words 'right' and 'wrong' in such a way that there is no contradiction in saying 'It would be wrong to do that (say, kill Aunt Martha who has left me a legacy) although it would be more advantageous to me than any other course open at the moment".[28]

226.   Can one quarrel with Baier's example? Many an Aunt Martha has been murdered in consequence of such reflections. There are, however, complications to be noted. First, for the murder to be to the homicidal nephew's advantage, it would have to be accomplished in a covert manner sufficient to avoid all associated legal and social sanctions. Secondly, and more importantly, one who reasons as the nephew at once demonstrates that he is an amoral or immoral person: certainly he is not committed to any moral principle that precludes killing anyone to acquire a legacy. When the nephew says, "It would be wrong to kill Aunt Martha", he is simply giving lip-service to a conception of being wrong; alternatively, one might say that he has a deplorably noncommittal conception of what is right and what is wrong: that, of course, is not uncommon today.

227.   Unfortunately, the fact of the matter is that some say "Yes, killing Aunt Martha would be morally wrong, but what has being moral done for me? I need the money." On the assumption that the

---

[28] *Op. cit.*, 7. A footnote, directing one to a later discussion of ethical egoism, has been omitted.

murder can be accomplished in a sufficiently covert manner, and assuming that the nephew is not troubled by moral commitments, killing Aunt Martha would seem to be to the nephew's advantage.

228.   Bentham, of course, would not have condoned the killing of Aunt Martha. After all, he would certainly have considered Aunt Martha's happiness as well as that of her homicidal nephew. But considering both the nephew's and Martha's happiness poses a problem.

229.   Relative to the happiness of the nephew, the principle of utility dictates that the action in question, the killing of Aunt Martha, would be right, or at least it would not be wrong. But relative to the happiness of Aunt Martha, the principle of utility dictates that the very same action, the killing of Aunt Martha, would be wrong, or at least it would not be right. Thus construed in reference to individuals, the principle of utility here leads to contradictory judgments about the rightness or wrongness of killing Aunt Martha.

230.   Suppose that instead of considering either individual, we consider the group constituted by the pair of individuals in question, the nephew and Aunt Martha. Would the killing of Aunt Martha and the consequent acquisition of the legacy by the nephew result in the greatest happiness of the group? Let us assume that the nephew would be quite happy and happier than before: what about Aunt Martha? Once she is dead, it would make no sense to speak of her as being happy or unhappy. Furthermore, once she is dead, the group of two is reduced to a group of one, namely, the nephew. The principle of utility would then here seem to dictate that, given our assumption about his consequent happiness, the nephew should kill Aunt Martha.

231.   It should be noted that it would make no difference if the group in question were trivially enlarged, say the nephew had various evil associates, all of whom would share in the legacy: the same conclusion would be forthcoming.

232.   Suppose we consider a different group, that constituted by the inmates and the warders of all our prisons: wouldn't it be for the greatest good of the greatest number of that population if the warders and inmates were to change places? Surely the happiness of that

population would be greatly increased if the warders were incarcerated and the inmates released. The principle of utility, if invoked in this case, would seem to dictate that such an exchange would be right, or at least, it would not be wrong. But it would, of course, be wrong, just as the killing of Martha would be wrong.

233.   It should be noted that such exchanges have, on a smaller scale, in fact occurred. Prisoners have captured their prison and incarcerated their warders. The reaction of the government was to bring in the army and return prisoners and warders to the original position. In so doing, the government was not acting in accordance with the principle of utility with respect to the limited population in question.

234.   There are, no doubt, indefinitely many populations and acts or actions with respect to which an appeal to the principle of utility would yield what many of us would accept as a correct judgment about the rightness or wrongness of the acts or actions; but just as surely there are indefinitely many populations and acts or actions with respect to which an appeal to the principle of utility would yield what many of us would take to be an incorrect judgment about the rightness or wrongness of the acts or actions.

235.   Perhaps the problem here is that we have focused on the wrong kind of group. Despite Bentham's own words, he was not truly concerned with the acts of individuals but with the acts of legislatures. He was primarily concerned, not with morality, but the law. As he somewhere remarked, "If the thunders of the law are of no avail, what can the whispers of morality achieve?" The acts of legislatures concern the society over which the legislature governs. Hence the relevant group is the society at large.

236.   The contrast, invoked here between the "individual" and the "society at large", was expressed by Bentham as a contrast between the individual and the "community". Unfortunately, he held a narrow mistaken reductionist view of the interest of the community: according to Bentham, the interest of the community is simply "the sum of the

interests of the several members who compose it."[29] Since the society at large, or, for that matter, the "community", has no determinate temporal boundaries, and no determinate number of members, there is no sense in speaking of "the sum of the interests of the several members who compose it". The mistake here arises from an unrealistic synchronic view of a society: societies, communities, are diachronic entities subject to continuous change.

237.   Construed in reference to the society at large, Bentham's principle directs one to be concerned with the greatest happiness of the greatest number of persons. That would be a sensible idea when it made sense, which it rarely does. In actual cases in the real world, an appeal to the principle of utility, when concerned with the society at large, is likely to be merely fatuous.

238.   Consider a case that occurred in Boston, in the 1950's: should Route 2, the major highway from the suburbs to the center city, be widened? There were reasons to do it: the flow of traffic would be increased, commuters would save about five minutes of travel time; business in the center city would presumably profit; and so forth. There were reasons not to do it: the widening of the highway would necessitate the destruction of fine old houses and fine old trees adjacent to the highway; there would be a considerable increase in the amount of traffic in the suburbs, suburbs such as Arlington, Belmont, Lexington and Concord; there would be a corresponding increase in the population density of the area, an increase in air-pollution and so on. In short, the ramifications were bound to be, and were, considerable.

239.   Which alternative would make the greater contribution to the greatest number? Here one must, in the name of good sense, realize that such a question is virtually senseless.

240.   The principle of utility requires that one count noses and assess the impact of the action on those noses; but which noses one is to

---

[29] *Op. cit.*, 3.

count, how one is to count them and how one is to assess the impact of the action has never been revealed.

241.   Do very young ones count more than very old ones, or very very old ones? Is a twenty five year old nose more sensitive than a sixty five year old nose, but, if so, how much more sensitive? Does one count green, puce, black, yellow, red and white alike? Personally, I am not overfond of puce. Does that matter? It may, if I am the one doing the counting. Is one to make amends for the poor or the black and blue? Does having been battered matter? Is a nearby nose more important than one far away?

242.   In counting noses, does one count those of the yet unborn? If so, how does one do that and how many are there?

243.   My great grandchildren, if there will be any, might be concerned to visit and view Lexington and Concord, both because of their place in American history and their place in my personal family history. The degradation of Lexington and Concord would not be to the interest of my as yet unborn great grandchildren. Of course if they never manage to be born then these considerations need not enter into our computations; but what the unborn will manage to do is something that I, not being a Utilitarian, would not know.

244.   Principles such as the principle of utility, when construed as applying to the society at large, are as useful in the real world as the principal rule of roulette: endeavor to place your money on the winning number.

245.   Bentham's "principle of utility" is, for me, and for reasons which by now may be evident, not a moral principle: it is best construed simply as a mild moral maxim to the effect that one should attend, in so far as it is possible and feasible, to the greatest good of individuals and of the society.

246.   I say "a mild moral maxim" because being to someone's advantage, or being prudent, or being expedient has nothing directly to do with morality. If doing something is to my advantage then I may have a reason to do it: it does not follow that I have a moral reason to do it. In a tennis match, it may be expedient that I serve directly into

the body of my opponent: I do not have any moral reason to do so. (And, of course, as I have already said, Bentham was not truly interested in morality: his *Introduction* was just that: an introduction to his *Limits of jurisprudence defined*[30]; prudence and jurisprudence were his genuine concerns.)

247.   Moral reasons stem from moral principles, moral commitments and moral concerns. They override and outweigh all considerations of expediency. Thus, even if it is expedient and to my considerable advantage that I do something that is to your disadvantage, depending on what is in question, I may have a moral reason not to do it. This is simply owing to the fact that I, as many others, am committed to the principle that one ought not do that which diminishes the happiness of others. This principle, as all sensible others, is, of course, subject to complex defeasibility conditions. Thus, for example, it doesn't follow that I have a moral reason not to attempt to win a tennis match even if my winning is likely to diminish the happiness of my opponent. It is part of the game to put oneself at risk: my opponent and I both understand that. On the other hand, there was an instance in which I did have a moral reason not to attempt to win a tennis match owing to the fact that I was playing with a child who would have been excessively distressed had he lost the match.

248.   To adhere to Bentham's principle of utility would be to confound morality on the basis of expediency.

> "They gathered a council, the Chief Priests and Pharisees, and said "What do we, for this man doth many miracles. If we let him alone so, all will believe in him and the Romans will come and take away our place and nation." But one of them, called Caïphas, being the high priest that year, prophesied saying "It is expedient for you that one man should die for the people and

---

[30] *Limits of jurisprudence defined* (University of London: Athlone Press, 1970). A cautionary note: One must take care in reading Bentham that one is, in fact, reading Bentham. He did not write the *Deontology*, or the *Handbook* or *The Principles of Legislation*: they were put together by other people from his papers.

that the whole nation perish not." From that day forward they
devised to put him to death".[31]

249.   I have said that Bentham's Principle of Utility is not a moral
principle, but, at best, a mild moral maxim. What is a moral principle?
That is a question we shall turn to later. First, however, we must
consider the conception of fairness.

250.   The conception invoked in the exhortation "Be fair!" is a
simple beast with a strong back and a weak mind; an athletic
conception, more emotive than cognitive. Despite the tiresome
propensity of those moralizing constantly to invoke it, the conception
of fairness is fit for use only in small and uncomplicated domains, say
a domain of children. But, in time, simple children grow into complex
adults: considerations of fairness are generally otiose in modern
populous complex societies.

251.   Having two chocolate bars to distribute and being confronted
with a pair of identical twins, identical in all the respects that they can
be identical in, and so each being equally desirous of chocolate, it
could be fair to give one to each, and it could be unfair to give two to
one and none to the other.

252.   The grades in a certain course are supposed to be determined
solely on the basis of the results of multiple choice tests. Two children
do equally well on the tests, but the instructor, being attracted to the
prettier of the two, gives her a higher grade than the other. Given that
prettiness is not a relevant consideration in grading, the instructor has
been, not only unfair, but unjust.

253.   A conception of fairness can sensibly be invoked only if
relevant parameters can be determined: one must determine relevant
considerations and a relevant domain. In the absence of such a
determination, an appeal to fairness is merely a rhetorical flourish.

---

[31] From "Collegerunt", a Gregorian Chant, translated by Thomas Merton (Father
Louis), from LAUDATE DOMINUM Gregorian Chant by The Trappist Monks,
Columbia Records ML 54394.

254. "Is it fair that this one be born ugly and that one beautiful?" "Is it fair for each state of the United States to be represented by the same number of senators in Washington?" Could the governor of California, for example, claim that considerations of fairness dictate that if North Dakota sends two senators to Washington, California should send four, or perhaps forty? Being a native New Yorker and having ten million dollars which he wished to dispose of philanthropically, and mistakenly assuming that there were only ten million people in New York, a man did his best to give one dollar each to ten million inhabitants of New York. When asked why he distributed the money in that stupid way, his response was that such a distribution was dictated by considerations of fairness. "Is it fair for the government to give money to people who are not working, but not to people who are?" "Is it fair to tax one man, X, at a rate of thirty five percent of his income, another, Y, at a rate of twenty percent of his income?". Of course, if what is in question is a graduated tax rate adjusted to income, X must have a greater income than Y, but what difference does that make with respect to fairness? Does it matter how hard X and Y work for their income? Is their psychology relevant?

255. I am not suggesting that there be no relief for the unemployed, nor that rich and poor be taxed at the same rate. But if the unemployed are to be helped, or the rich and poor not to be taxed at the same rate, it is not because of considerations of fairness.

256. John Rawls claims otherwise:

"The social consequences of any one person (perhaps even many people) not paying his tax are unnoticeable, and let us suppose zero in value, but there is a noticeable private gain for the person himself, or for another to whom he chooses to give it (the institution of income tax is subject to the first kind of instability). The duty of fair play binds us to pay our tax, nevertheless, since we have accepted, and intend to continue doing so, the benefits of the fiscal system to which the income tax belongs. Why is this reasonable and not a blind following of a rule, when a greater net sum of advantages is possible? - because the system of cooperation consistently followed by everyone else itself produces the advantages generally enjoyed and in the case of a practice such as the income tax there is no reason to give exemptions to anyone so that they might enjoy the possible benefit. (An analogous case is the moral obligation to vote and so to work the constitutional procedure from which one has benefited....)"[32]

257.   (I have here avoided references to Rawls' *A Theory of Justice* for, though I believe essentially the same views are stated there, I see no need to become entangled in a discussion of what he calls "the original position". For example, he there says "..., unjust social arrangements are themselves a kind of extortion, even violence, and consent to them does not bind. The reason for this condition is that the parties in the original position would insist upon it." 343.)

258.   Is this true: "... the system of cooperation consistently followed by everyone else itself produces the advantages generally enjoyed"? I think not.

259.   What in fact produces whatever is in fact produced is the system of cooperation more or less consistently followed by a considerable number of persons, a very considerable number of persons, but not followed by a considerable number of others.

260.   The problem of free-riders is generally mischaracterized as the problem of "the free-rider".

261.   Nonpayment of income tax and nonvoting are not analogous in critical respects. Voting procedures supply information, which information could, conceivably, be equally well supplied by some sort of samples. Since, in fact, a considerable percentage of the eligible population fails to cast a vote in national elections, all that is ever actually in question, anyway, is some sort of degenerate sample. Furthermore, since what is in question is a large state with a population of over 200 million, any statement about or in reference to

---

[32] John Rawls, "Legal Obligation and the Duty of Fair Play" in Sidney Hook ed., *Law And Philosophy: A Symposium* (New York: New York University Press, 1964).

that population must be of an essentially statistical character based on what is whimsically characterized as a "sampling" technique. In so far as the population of the country is not accessible to examination, there is no clear sense in which one's "sample" can be held to be representative. Indeed, in so far as one knows that voting behavior is governed by all sorts of factors, economic, geographical and meteorological, one knows that no such "sample" can possibly be deemed representative. Thus there is no clear sense in which what one is dealing with can sensibly be characterized as a "sample". Even so, if some sort of information acquiring procedure were developed, there might then be no need for citizens to vote. No tax "sample" could similarly supply the same monies.

262.   All votes are equal: not all tax returns are equal. The loss of revenue resulting from the nonpayment of taxes by a single enormously wealthy individual could be socially significant. Of course, given the tax loop-holes available to the rich, tax free bonds and so forth, possibly the nonpayment of taxes by even an enormously wealthy individual need not be significant.

263.   Once one is rid of the untrue, but wonderfully simplifying, assumption that "everyone else" pays his taxes, the problem posed by free-riders is no longer amenable to the simple solution supposedly provided by an appeal to a duty of "fair play". "Is it fair that I not enjoy the benefits that accrue to free-riders when so many do? Why should I be so deprived?"

264.   Despite current views to the contrary, there is no need to confuse a conception of fairness with a conception of justice. Justice is an institutional conception, fairness pertains primarily to individual interrelations. Considerations of fairness can readily conflict with considerations of justice.

265.   Two men of equal age are each convicted of the same crime: each committed armed robbery; each is sentenced to ten years in the same state penitentiary. What could be fairer? Nonetheless, one is, and the other is not, thereby subjected to what some, and I for one, would deem to be an enormous injustice. One is a handsome, slender, somewhat effeminate looking young man; the other is a powerful

macho body building type. The former is virtually certain to be raped, sodomized; the latter is likely to be untouched.

266.   The same period of incarceration for each in the same penitentiary cannot, in itself, be deemed unfair. But the realities of the matter are such that one is virtually condemned to death, the other to perhaps less than ten years in prison, assuming time off for good behavior. According to my conception of justice, such a virtual sentence of death would be unjust.

267.   If, however, aware of the realities of the matter, a judge were to impose unequal sentences, say, by sending the weaker of the two to a minimum security prison with more docile inmates, the other felon could rightly maintain that he was being treated unfairly. So there is a judicial choice: be fair but unjust or be just but unfair.

268.   The institutional character of justice is well marked in the traditional archetypal image: a blindfolded woman carrying a scale in one hand, a sword in the other. Those preoccupied with a conception of justice as fairness fail to see the sword, the symbol of institutionalized authority.

269.   There is no such duty as "the duty of fair play" that binds us to pay our taxes.[33] Paying taxes may be a game for some, those who can afford to play games with the Internal Revenue Service, but that is a privilege reserved for the rich or the powerful.

270.   A citizen of a democracy, such as that enjoyed here in America, has a civic duty to pay his taxes: whether or not others do their duty has nothing to do with the matter. And such a citizen also has a civic duty to vote: again, whether or not others do their duty has nothing to do with the matter.

271.   A citizen who fails to pay his taxes, or who fails to vote, fails to do his duty. In failing to do his duty he may or may not be acting immorally, but he is not being unfair.

---

[33] With respect to a difference between "fair play" and "fair dealing", *cf.* J. P. Day, "Fairness And Fortune", *The Philosopher's Annual*, ed. by D. L. Boyer, P. Grim and J. T. Sanders (Towota, New Jersey: Rowman & Littlefield, 1978) 48.

272.   Whether or not a failure to pay taxes, or a failure to vote, is an immoral act depends on various factors: the morality of the society in question, the person's own morality, the precise character of the act, the actual temporal social significance of the act, the person's circumstances, and so on. Thus although every citizen has a civic duty to vote, it does not follow that every citizen has a moral obligation to vote. One can hardly urge a member of an oppressed minority to vote on the grounds that there is a constitutional procedure from which he has "benefited". Nor can one urge a member of an oppressed minority to pay his taxes on the ground that he has accepted "the benefits of the fiscal system to which the income tax belongs." If one wanders through the ghettoes of our great cities, rats and feces are more in evidence than fiscal benefits.

273.   There is no such duty as "the duty of fair play".

274.   In playing tennis without the aid of lines persons, a player is obliged to make the line calls on his own side of the net. He is under a social obligation to give correct calls to the best of his ability. The rule is that when one is in doubt, the benefit of the doubt is to be given to one's opponent. So if the player is uncertain whether his opponent's ball was in or out, if he has the call, he must call it in. (It is not correct, as some club players are wont to do, to call a let, a replay of the point.)

275.   One has an obligation, one is under an obligation, one is obliged to make calls in a certain way. There is, however, no need to confuse or conflate obligations and duties: a player does not have a duty to make calls, or a duty to make calls in a certain way. If there were lines persons, they would have the duty of making line calls. But players, owing to the lack of lines persons, though perhaps obliged to make line calls do not, *ipso facto*, have a duty to make such calls.

276.   Do I have a duty to respect other persons? Do I have a duty to help a person in distress? What is the difference between saying that one ought to respect other persons or that one ought to help a person in distress, and saying that one has a duty to do such things?

277.   In common usage, a duty is an obligatory service. If one is hired for a certain position, one may ask "What are my duties? What am I obliged to do?".

278.   It may be true that I ought to respect other persons, that I ought to help a person in distress. But from that it does not follow that I am obliged to do either. Hence, if it is my duty to do these things, it is not simply because I ought to do these things.

279.   What if I am obliged to respect other persons or I am obliged to help a person in distress? For if I am not so obliged, I can have no such duties. But even if I am obliged to do these things, does it follow that I have a duty to do these things? One can grant that any obligatory service is a duty without granting that one has such duties as these.

280.   Giving respect or aid to others is not rendering a service. If someone walking in my garden picked up and disposed of a bit trash that he came across while walking, he did me a service, but the service he did me is not like that rendered by the gardener hired to tend the garden.

281.   Consider the social obligation not to urinate on one's host's table cloth while at dinner: an absurd obligation no doubt, but an obligation nonetheless. Do I have a duty not to behave in such a manner? I certainly would not say so. But why not?

282.   I think one must, or I must, or at any rate I will, hold on to the original thread of duty: a duty is an obligatory service, and service, in its relevant sense, is an institutional conception. The title of Bradley's famous essay is altogether apt: "My station and its duties": for duties arise from a position, a station, a role in a group or a society.

283.   There is no such role as the role of the nonurinator; nor is there such a role as a respecter of other persons: but is there such a role as an aider of persons in distress? In Orange County, North Carolina, there is a public service organization, the Orange County Rescue Squad. It is the duty of the members of this admirable organization to aid persons in distress. If in distress and adjacent to a telephone, all one need do is dial 911, detail one's problem, and aid is on its way.

But I am not a member of the Orange County Rescue Squad: do I have any such duty? I see no reason to believe it.

284.   To be a member of the human race is not, *ipso facto*, to have a role to play.

285.   (The above discussion is not offered as, nor should it be read as, a substantive criticism of John Rawls's impressive and profound *Theory of Justice*. I am not attempting to fault Rawls's conception of "justice as fairness", particularly when it is interpreted in terms of his essay "Justice as Fairness: Political not Metaphysical", *Philosophy and Public Affairs*, Summer 1985, Vol. 14, No. 3, 223-251. My quarrel here is, in part, linguistic; I am concerned with what I take to be inappropriate or loose or deviant uses of the words 'fair', 'play', and 'duty'. But this is not to say that all issues raised are linguistic: for example, the problem of free-riders is not; neither is the futility of the attempt to slide from civic duty to moral obligation on the basis of a nonexistent "duty of fair play" simply a matter of semantics.)

286.   Previously I said that a citizen who fails to pay his taxes, or who fails to vote, fails to do his duty. In failing to do his duty he may or may not be acting immorally, but he is not being unfair. To suppose that one who fails to do his duty is being unfair is to suppose that what others do is directly and immediately relevant to whether or not the person has a certain duty or is under a certain obligation. Of course, this is sometimes so, depending on precisely what obligation is in question. There are, however, all sorts of obligations with respect to which what others do, or would do, is wholly irrelevant.

287.   "What if everyone were to do that?" is a familiar question too often put by persons in moral discourse who appear to lust after generality: one is somehow supposed to put this question to oneself in the course of electing to perform some act or action.

288.   The never-never-landish aspect of the principles, maxims, and injunctions that some are prone to promulgate is well displayed in this remarkable question, to which the answer may well be "Something absurd or terrible", regardless of the innocence of the act.

289.   Someone litters, drops some trash on a much frequented public beach.

> "... if we try saying "How would it be for you if everyone behaved like that?" he [the amoral person] will reply, "Well, if they did, not good, I suppose - though in fact I might do better in the resulting chaos than some of the others. But the fact is that most of them are not going to do so; and if they do ever get round to it, I shall be dead by then." The appeal to the consequences of an *imagined* universalization is an essentially moral argument, and he [the amoral person] is, consistently, not impressed by it"[34]

290.   What would happen if everyone trashed the beach? The beach would be devastated. What does that prove? Only that it would be absurd to heed such an enjoinder as "Everyone should trash the beach". Other than that, it proves nothing at all. Of course the person ought not to litter, ought not to trash a public beach. But the reason why he ought not has nothing to with the fact that if everyone were to do what he did, the beach would be devastated.

291.   I play tennis at two o'clock on a hot August day. What would happen if everyone were to do, or try to do, that? There wouldn't be enough courts; the roads leading to the courts would be snarled in traffic jams; thousands and thousands of the feeble would die of heat prostration and cardiac arrest; and no one would be minding the store, tending patients and so forth. Again, I go jogging: what would happen if everyone were to do, or try to do, that? Again, a disaster, for thousands and thousands would die in the streets, while patients, left alone, unattended, would die in their beds, or in the course of futile efforts to go jogging. And anyway, there wouldn't be any place or space to jog in. Places like Tokyo already have wall-to-wall humanity.

---

[34] Bernard Williams, *op. cit.*, 4.

292. If the question is to make any sense, perhaps the scope of the term 'everyone' must be drastically restricted. But even that cannot salvage this absurd query.

293. I am in New York City and I take a shower at 4:00 a.m. Excluding sick-bed patients, doctors engaged in their practice, morticians at work and so on, what if everyone in New York were to take a shower at 4:00 am? There would be an instant crisis at the city water department.

294. Of course, such crises never occur. The people at the water department know that not everyone in New York will take a shower at 4:00 am. What if it were to become the general practice of New Yorkers to take a shower at 4:00 a.m.? Then there would be a radical alteration in the behavior of the people. Apart from the fact that they might be somewhat cleaner, I cannot even guess what significant consequences such a practice might have.

295. There is another aspect of the query, "What if everyone were to do that?", that must be noted. To ask what would happen if everyone were to perform that act or action may be thought to be a way of asking whether the particular act or action is in compliance with and in conformance to a particular morality, and, if so, whether there is some relevant covering enjoinder, which the act in question is in conformance to, that admits of some sort of universalization. But universalization has different aspects and the futility of the query remains.

296. Consider playing tennis again: I elect to play tennis on hard courts on an August afternoon when the air temperature is 95 Fahrenheit, the court surface is about 118 Fahrenheit. What if everyone were to do that? It would, of course, be a disaster: enormous numbers of persons would die of heat prostration, cardiac arrest and so forth. But what is the relevant enjoinder? Is it (1)?

(1) Everyone should play tennis on hard courts in the August heat.

297. That would, of course, be a ridiculous enjoinder. It does not merely allow but directly calls for what would be a disaster if the

enjoinder were generally complied with. A relevant, and sensible, covering enjoinder could be:

> (2) All persons have the right to play on hard courts in the August heat.

The associated precept might be:

> (3) No persons are to be prevented from playing on hard courts in the August heat without good and sufficient reason.

298.   I see no reason to object to either (2) or (3) despite the fact that if everyone were to exercise the right to play tennis on hard courts in the August heat, it would be a disaster.

299.   That, in some, but of course not all, cases everyone has the right to do what I do, when what I do is not wrong, is one thing: that everyone should do what I do is a totally different matter.

300.   Suppose I see an overweight type obviously in no condition to be running around a tennis court in the August heat. Should I attempt to prevent him from playing? If I were to say to him "You should realize that what you are doing may be hazardous to your health", he might well reply "Mind your own business!" Am I then physically to prevent him? That might prove hazardous to both his and my health. Do I have good and sufficient reason to prevent him from playing? I do not. I have some reason, for I do believe that what he is doing is hazardous to his health. But that is hardly sufficient reason for me, a total stranger, to interfere with his exercise of his right to play when he chooses to do so. Of course the obese type ought not to be doing what he is doing. But I cannot deny that he has the right to be a fool if he so chooses. It is not that I am not my brother's keeper, but that I am not my brother's dictator. Fortunately, few of the physically unfit elect to play tennis in the August heat, and a natural disaster awaits those that do.

301.   The moral of all this should be reasonably clear: questions of universality may have, at least, two distinct aspects. A statement of a right may have universal scope in that it may apply to all persons, even though the universal exercise of that right may prove to be something disastrous. The query "What would happen if everyone did that?"

directs one to consider the imagined universalization of some act or action. With respect to a familiar morality, everyone has the right to play tennis in the August heat; no one has the right to litter. Imagined universalizations of either act are simply morally irrelevant.

302. One need not confuse the universal scope of a right with a universal exercise of that right. There are all sorts of rights such that the universal exercise of that right might provoke a disaster. In America, everyone has the right to withdraw all his or her monies from any banks in which they have been deposited. If everyone in America were simultaneously to exercise that right, the country would probably suffer an economic collapse.

303. More generally, attention to the consequences of the universal exercise of a right may well be beyond the scope of a rational morality. Any morality is inevitably limited. The need for attention to all possible consequences of compliance with or conformance to that morality is a metaphysical myth, its possibility, a metaphysical dream.

304. No morality can rationally be conceived of as having a genuinely universal range of application in that it is concerned with and attends to all possible contingencies. One need only look to language, any language, and the diachronic evolution of that language, to see the absurdity of attempting to accommodate all unlikely or unknown or future contingencies. The lexicon of any language is in constant fluctuation. Such a fluctuation is the reflection of the changing concerns of the speakers of the language. The moral concerns of today need not be those of tomorrow. The moral precepts of today may have no relevance, no application, to the problems of tomorrow. At its best, any morality is an organic, conceptual and regulative instrument subject to growth, maturation and inevitable decay. That it be adequate to the day is all that one can reasonably require.

"If it be right that the conduct of the 19th century should be determined not by its own judgment but by that of the 18th, it will be equally right that the conduct of the 20th century should be determined not by its own judgment but by that of the 19th. The same principle still pursued, what at length would be the consequence? In the process of time the practice of legislation would be at an end: the conduct and fate of all men would be determined by those who neither knew nor cared anything about the matter. The aggregate body of the living would then remain forever in subjection to an inexorable tyranny exercised, as it were, by the aggregate body of the dead".[35]

305.   Previously I said that Bentham's Principle of Utility is not a moral principle but, at best, a mild moral maxim. In contrast, it will help, and is now time, to consider a genuine and important moral principle, namely, "All persons have the right to liberty". So it is said, but what is being said?

306.   Some, possibly not many, would say this: "It is always wrong to deprive any person of his or her liberty." But what about felons, murderers, the criminally insane, what about persons convicted and incarcerated? Do they have the right to liberty? And some might respond: "Even these are not rightly, not justly, imprisoned; or if "justly imprisoned" then "justice" here is only a matter of expediency, has itself no other justification." Thus, the principle is construed rigidly, without exceptions or qualifications or defeasibility conditions. In the same vein, Kant, caught in a vice of virtue, insisted on the truth, no matter what.

307.   Immanuel Kant claimed that "to tell a falsehood to a murderer who asked us whether our friend, of whom he was in pursuit, had not taken refuge in our house, would be a crime".[36] Kant's principal statement in support of this claim was this:

> "... by making a false statement ... I do wrong to men in general in the most essential point of duty, so that it may be called a lie

---

[35] Jeremy Bentham, *Bentham's Handbook of Political Fallacies* ed. by H. A. Larrabee (Baltimore: The Johns Hopkins Press, 1952) 56.

[36] *Cf.* I. Kant, *Critique of Practical Reason and Other Works on the Theory of Ethics*, trans. by Thomas Kingsmill Abbott (London: Longmans, Green and Co. Ltd., 6th ed. 1909, reprinted 1963) Appendix 361.

(though not in the jurist's sense), that is, so far as in me lies I cause that declarations in general find no credit, and hence all rights founded on contract should lose their force; and this is a wrong which is done to mankind".[37]

308.   Does my telling a lie "cause that declarations in general find no credit"? Does my vote cause a national president to be elected? Can my single vote effect the outcome of an American national presidential election? In one way, yes; in another, no.

309.   My single vote does, and so can, increase the plurality of the candidate I vote for. My single vote has no effect whatever in determining the winner of the election. No American presidential candidate ever has, or could be, elected by a single popular vote in a national election. Insufficient pluralities invariably call for recounts, and if the pluralities remain insufficient, elections are rerun.

310.   To what extent do I cause a national presidential candidate to be elected? To none at all.

311.   If I lie, to what extent do I "cause that declarations in general find no credit"? To none at all: unfortunately, ordinary individuals have no such causal efficacy. "If my vote has no causal efficacy then neither has yours and neither has anyone's: who then elected the president?" An American national president is elected by a very large group of persons: the causal efficacy of the group is not the cumulative sum of the causal efficacy of each member of the group.[38]

312.   Not only is it not true that if I lie, "I cause that declarations in general find no credit", not even my own declarations need, in general, lose their credibility. It depends on what one lies about and on where and when and why and how and to whom one lies. It also depends on whether the lie is ever discovered to be a lie. The extreme unreality of

---

[37] *Op. cit.*, 362.

[38] For an analog of this claim in statistical theory, see Elliot M. Cramer "Significance Tests and Tests of Models in Multiple Regression", *The American Statistician*, October 1972, Vol. 26, No. 4. In particular, see situation "3) $R2$ but none of the βi significant."

Kant's claim should be, must be, if one is to get moral matters right, appreciated.

313.   Kant was doubly in error: here he apparently failed to consider either persons or numbers.

314.   The human psyche is as variegated and complex in color and character as the most exotic work of art or the most spectacular heterogeneous ensemble of garbage. If I say, to a friend who is ill and who looks like death, "You look fine today", that in no way undermines the credibility of my aesthetic, or political, or moral declarations. He, knowing that I lie, nonetheless attends to what I say and, if only for a moment, may feel the better for it. This is an instance, not of motivated irrationality but, rather, of a rational suspension of customary critical attitudes governing the giving of credence: a constant unflagging commitment to truth would call for an incredible constitution.

315.   Perhaps it is conceivable that there be a society in which, if everyone always spoke only the truth, it would be good: but I cannot conceive of it. What sort of persons could form such a society? Mankind cannot stand too much reality. It would be easier for one to tell the truth if another could bear to hear it. Telling the truth is an easy way to maximize misery. To one who looked terrible and asked "How do I look?", one concerned to speak only the truth could say "You look terrible", which could well have the effect of making him look and feel even more dreadful. Doctors might say to some "You have an incurable ailment: you will die an agonizing death", so supplementing future agony with instant anxiety. There would be no soothing bolstering face saving lies for the dying, the frustrated, the incompetent, the retarded, the disadvantaged.

316.   There is an enormous conceptual chasm that separates problems concerned with small numbers of people from problems concerned with large numbers. To this, apparently, Kant gave no attention. It may make good sense to say that there are exactly three people in a certain room. It does not make good sense to say that there are exactly 240,000,023 people in the United States.

317.   Given various social institutions, one may have an obligation to cast a vote. The single vote of an Athenian citizen may have been of appreciable significance: the single vote of an average American citizen in a national election is of absolutely minimal significance. It is of no significance whatever in determining the outcome of a national American presidential election: it has some slight effect in that it can augment the plurality of a candidate. The fact of the matter is that the effect of a single vote asymptotically approaches zero as the number of voters increases.

318.   Thus one cannot escape the conclusion that, in this democracy, it is my civic duty to perform an act almost devoid of significance. Almost, but not quite: One must grant that the casting of a single vote has, anyway, and at least, a purely symbolic significance: it is a symbolic gesture in support of the democratic process. Symbol minded behavior is often suspect, but it cannot be ignored.

319.   It is also the fact of the matter that my telling a lie has zero effect on the reliability of declarations in general.

320.   Compare the moral principle expressed by (T) with statement (S):

(T) All persons should always speak the truth.

(S) All persons should sometimes speak the truth and sometimes not.

321.   Kant accepted formulation (T) and construed it rigidly, in robot fashion. Possibly he was impelled to do so by the conviction that (S) would be the only available alternative to (T) and that the principle expressed by (S) would be an untenable moral principle. In insisting that Kant was in error, however, I am not urging a commitment to (S). According to many moralities, and mine for one, a commitment to (S) as a moral principle would be a serious moral error. But nothing compels the Kantian construal: one can accept formulation (T) and yet not agree with Kant. One can readily construe (T) as a reasonable formulation and expression of an important regulative instrument. One who is committed to (T), so construed, always has a reason to tell the truth. If he lies, he must have good and sufficient reason to lie, reason

weighty enough to outweigh the reason provided by principle (T) for telling the truth.

322.   A reason for compliance with and conformance to (T), construed as a regulative instrument, is indicated in Kant's discussion:

> "For instance, if you have *by a lie* hindered a man who is even now planning a murder, you are legally responsible for all the consequences. But if you have strictly adhered to the truth, public justice can find no fault with you, be the unforeseen consequence what it may. It is possible that whilst you have honestly answered Yes to the murderer's question, whether his intended victim is in the house, the latter may have gone out unobserved, and so not have come in the way of the murderer, and the deed therefore have not been done; whereas, if you lied and said he was not in the house, and he had really gone out (though unknown to you), so that the murderer met him as he went, and executed his purpose on him, then you might with justice be accused as the cause of his death. For if you had spoken the truth as well as you knew it, perhaps the murderer while seeking for his enemy in the house might have been caught by neighbors coming up and the deed prevented. Whoever then *tells a lie*, however good his intentions may be, must answer for the consequences of it, even before the civil tribunal, and must pay the penalty for them, however unforeseen they may have been".[39]

323.   The claim is that one cannot be faulted for telling the truth, but one is responsible for the consequences of telling a lie.

324.   Though Kant's claim is, again, exaggerated, there is some truth in it. For one who complies with and conforms to principle (T), construed as a regulative instrument, lies are always, as lies, morally suspect, always require exoneration, which is not to deny that their exoneration need not be explicit, may be only implicit in the context:

---

[39] *Op. cit.*, 363.

in contrast, truths are not always morally suspect and do not always require exoneration.

325.   To tell a lie to the would-be murderer would not be a crime: to tell the truth would be. The only redeeming feature of telling such a truth would be that it would constitute a symbolic gesture in support of a moral principle. But in insisting on telling the truth to the would-be murderer, Kant was being over symbol minded.

326.   Some cling to iron clad principles that absolutely prescribe, dictate, a certain course of action, principles laid down in advance of and without consideration of circumstances, principles that hold no matter what. Such principles might be called "robot principles", for those who would hold to such principles are "would-be robots". One can hold to such principles: there are would-be robots.

327.   Alternatively, some would say: "All persons have the right to liberty, but there are certain classes of cases in which this principle does not hold; for example, the case of the criminal, and there are other exceptions which one must learn to recognize."

"Thus, far from principles like 'Never say what is false' being in some way by nature irredeemably loose, it is part of our moral development to turn them from provisional principles into precise principles with their exceptions definitely laid down; this process is, of course, never completed, but it is always going on in any individual lifetime".[40]

328.   So construed, the principle "All persons have the right to liberty" is a general principle, one that admits of exceptions, exceptions that are to be detailed in the course of time.

329.   "All persons, except criminals": but which criminals, even those who have been released from prison? "All persons, except criminals not released from prison": but what if the criminal has not been released from prison solely because he is in the prison hospital, is too ill to be released? What if a criminal has been released from prison

---

[40] R. M. Hare, *The Language of Morals*, (Oxford: Clarendon Press, 1961) 54.

but breaks the law anew? What if he is only suspected of breaking the law? Does he then not have the right to liberty?

330.   This is much like the law: adding qualifications to statements, making general statements more and more specific, enumerating the various possibilities likely to occur, reviewing and explicitly accounting for diverse complications apt to be encountered in practice. If one stares hard at the law, focuses one's eye on legalistic qualifications, on characteristically legal procedures, one is then strongly inclined, when confronted with a statement like "All persons have the right to liberty," to construe it as a crude grotesquely imprecise form of a legal statement. So Bentham construed it, and, so construed, it is deserving of Bentham's criticism. Construed in a legal manner, as a merely general principle, "All persons have the right to liberty" is, as Halifax said, a "coarse thing".

331.   Consider statement (I):

> (I) Students are not allowed to leave the class room during class hours.

(I) is a statement of a regulation concerned with and governing the conduct of students; it is a directive to refrain from a certain course of action. Contrast (I) with (II):

> (II) Students are not allowed to leave the class room during class hours, except on Fridays.

332.   In (II), the clause, "except on Fridays," explicitly indicates that the regulation is not concerned with what occurs during class hours on Fridays; thus the clause tends to limit the scope of the regulation. If regulation (I) was designed to prevent a general exodus from class owing to boredom on Mondays through Thursdays, but not on Fridays, and if such an exodus was completely ignored by the authorities if it occurred on Fridays, but was severely punished if it occurred on Mondays through Thursdays, and so forth, one could then sensibly claim that (II) was a more precise statement of the regulation than (I).

333.   But what if the building is on fire? Would (III)

(III) Students are not allowed to leave the class room during class hours, except on Fridays and except in the case of fire.

be more precise than (II)? But then, what about earthquakes, illness, the presence of poison gas, mice, crocodiles, a saber-tooth tiger, for all these are classes of cases?[41]

334.   One good reason for leaving the class room could be that the room was on fire, or that there were crocodiles roaming the room and so forth: there is no end to the number of good reasons there could be to leave the class room during the class hour.

335.   But not any reason for leaving need here be a good reason; that the teacher is boring is not apt to be, though it could, of course, be a good reason from another point of view, from the student's point of view. It is not apt to be a good reason, or if good, still not a sufficient reason here, because such a regulation might well be explicitly designed to prevent a general exodus owing to boredom during the class hour.

336.   Contrast (II) with (III): the fact that it is Friday, unlike the fact that the room is on fire, is not a reason, much less a good reason, to leave the class room.

337.   Suppose regulation (II) is in force. One who left the class room during class hours on Monday because he was bored would have broken the regulation. He would, accordingly, be subject to whatever penalties one incurs for such violations. What if he left because of fire? Has he broken the regulation? Would he be subject to penalties?

338.   He might be. If the regulation were enforced in robot fashion, he would be. But, ordinarily, his behavior could not be characterized as "an infraction of the regulation", and even if it were, no penalties would be apt to be forthcoming.

339.   If one insists, one can say that the regulation "does not apply" in the case of fire, this on the analogy with "The regulation does not

---

[41] See Paul Ziff, *Understanding Understanding* (Ithaca: Cornell University Press, 1966) Chapter VIII: "Something About Conceptual Schemes".

apply on Fridays"; but the way in which the regulation "does not apply" in the case of fire is radically different from the way in which it does not, in fact, apply on Fridays.

340.   Let regulation (II) be in force. Even so, that it is Friday during class hour is not a reason either to leave or not to leave the class room.

341.   A regulation cannot create reasons, cannot make what is not a reason a reason. What if one were to change the regulation by deleting the clause excepting Fridays, thus instituting regulation (I): has one therewith transmuted the fact that it is Friday during class hour into a reason? One can invent rules and regulations, and one can put them into practice; but to speak of inventing reasons is to speak of practicing to deceive. To create a reason would be more than a miracle.

342.   That a child is offered a reward, e.g., is promised a trip to the beach, if it practices the piano, may be a reason for the child to practice; thus in offering the reward, I have provided the child with a reason to practice. But I did not make it a reason. A reward is, for a child, a fairly good reason to practice. I offered the reward because such a reward is a reason to practice; if a reward were not a reason to practice, there would have been no sense in offering it. But I did not and could not make it a reason. No one can do that.

343.   The fact that it is Monday during class hour is not a reason not to leave the class room, but there is a reason not to leave the class room during class hour on Monday. The reason is simply this: it is against the regulation. That is, in itself, a reason.

344.   It would not be a reason if the regulation were not in force and was not enforced, for it is that that gives the regulation its force. No one makes this reason a reason: it simply is a reason. And because it is a reason, there is sense in having rules and regulations. If this reason were not a reason, rules and regulations could accomplish nothing, would be utterly pointless.

345.   The fact that it is Monday during class hour is not a reason not to leave the class room, but the fact that leaving the class room on Monday during class hour is against the regulation is a reason not to

leave the room on Monday during class hour. Furthermore, the statement of the regulation, (II), does not say there is a reason why students are not allowed to leave, though there may be a reason why such a regulation was instituted; but even if there is no good reason, or no reason at all, why the regulation was instituted, the regulation, nonetheless, provides reason, and, on occasion, a good reason, not to leave the class room during class hours on Mondays through Thursdays. But the regulation does not say there is such a reason, it does not report about a reason: it provides a reason.

346.   By creating rules and regulations one can, and often does, provide, not create, not report about, reasons for adopting or refraining from adopting certain courses of action.

347.   But what if the room is filled with a noxious gas? Rather than say "The regulation does not apply in such a case", one can more sensibly say that, in such a case, there is a reason to leave the room that overrides, not the regulation, but the reasons provided by the regulation. There would then be a reason, a good and sufficient reason, to leave the room. Reasons can enter into conflict with, can compete, with other reasons, can on occasion be overweighed by other reasons, can and must on occasion give way to other reasons.

348.   It is not that the regulation does not apply, not that the regulation is overridden, for if that were the case, there would be no reasons to override, to outweigh. It is, rather, that the reasons provided by the regulation are outweighed by other factors.

349.   Principles and regulations may be construed in robot fashion; so construed, they simply dictate acts or actions; if "Students are allowed ..." then never prevent it, no matter what; if "Students are not allowed ..." then never allow it, no matter what. Robots in striving for a mechanical paradise are more apt to create an automatic hell.

350.   Principles may be construed in a legal manner as merely general statements, admitting of exception without end; if so, they proscribe or prescribe acts or actions, but that vaguely, ineffectually, imprecisely.

351.   But moral principles can also be construed as regulative instruments, having a distinctive regulative function: they have the function, not of prescribing or proscribing acts or actions, but of either providing or undermining reasons for the performance, or the nonperformance, of various acts or actions.

352.   "All persons have the right to liberty" can be understood as a regulative instrument whose main function is to undermine reasons for depriving a person, any person, of his or her liberty. It need admit of no exceptions whatever. So understood, to say that all persons have the right to liberty is to say that no person should be deprived of his or her liberty without good and sufficient reason.

353.   "All persons have the right to liberty" is just one example of the statement of a moral principle: there are many others of precisely the same logical form. "Thou shalt not kill" is an excellent enjoinder that, unfortunately, is largely ignored throughout the world. It nonetheless serves to express a fundamental moral principle: it is wrong to kill anything. ("Anything", of course, here means any living thing: bacteria, cells, weeds, insects and even people.)

354.   This principle is related to a well-known Judaic-Christian commandment, but it has also been promulgated by other religious sects. As with all principles, it can, in Kantian robot fashion, be construed rigidly: the most ardent and conspicuous rigid construal of that principle would seem to have been supplied by the Jains of India. Devout Jains would not brush their teeth or wash their clothes; indeed, Maha-vira, a leader of the sect, along with many of his followers adopted the practice of going naked, for fear of killing some living thing. For a devout Jain, nothing could count as a sufficient reason to kill anything. Unsurprisingly, they practiced asceticism and self mortification.

355.   One of my moral principles is "It is wrong to kill anything", which, for me, is to say that absolutely nothing should be killed without good and sufficient reason. Principles of this form are clearly defeasible in that, even though they appear absolutely to prescribe or proscribe certain acts or actions, their genuine function is to provide reasons to perform or not perform the acts or actions in question,

which reasons may, in any given case, be overridden by other weightier reasons. Thus even though I may eat a carrot, and thus kill living cells, in doing so, I still stick with the principle: one must eat in order to survive. Analogously, I will, in self defense, swat a mosquito that attacks me. On the other hand, if a fly has somehow managed to enter and be trapped inside my screened in deck, I capture it and release it outside. I do not have any warrant to kill it. (I would consider that "an act of murder": of course, my rhetoric here is designed to display my own personal values which I wish others would share.)

356. There is, however, a profound dissimilarity between regulations, such as those governing behavior in classrooms, and moral principles. Regulations can be in force and can be enforced. Hence there need be no mystery about how they manage to provide reasons for performing or not performing various acts or actions. Moral principles cannot be similarly characterized. They are not literally in force, neither are they literally enforced. The force of moral principles then, their power, their efficacy, wants explaining.

357. To appreciate and understand the efficacy of moral principles, one must also appreciate the futility of attempting to formulate precise, nontrivial, nondefeasible and yet sensible moral principles. This should be apparent to anyone who appreciates the common conception of a promise.

358. Prichard said:

> "In promising, agreeing, or undertaking to do some action we seem to be creating or bringing into existence the obligation to do it, so much so that promising seems just to *be* binding ourselves, *i.e.* making ourselves bound, to do it, and the statement 'I ought to keep a promise', like 'I ought not to steal', seems a mere pleonasm.

> Yet an obligation seems a fact of a kind which it is impossible to create or bring into existence. There are, no doubt, certain facts which we do seem able to create. If, e.g., I make someone angry, I appear to bring into existence the fact that he is angry. But the fact that I am bound to do some action seems no more

one of these than does the fact that the square of three is odd".[42]

359.   Prichard's remarks are concerned with a particular social practice: the familiar practice of making promises. In referring to the familiar practice of promise making, I am referring to my local version of a relatively complex social practice that is, by and large, cross-culturally identifiable. I am assuming that the reader is more or less familiar with the practice that I am referring to: even if a reader is not familiar with what I am referring to, the discussion should serve to delineate the salient and relevant features of that practice. The term 'practice', as I am using it, is not, as it were, heavily theory laden.[43]

360.   With respect to familiar practice, if, for example, I promised to meet someone to perform some act then I am bound, morally bound, to perform that act. This, of course, does not mean that my promise cannot be subject to defeasibility conditions. If I fail to perform the promise, I may have a legitimate excuse that exonerates me from moral blame. But then again, I may not. And what counts as a legitimate excuse, or even whether anything is a legitimate excuse, depends on the morality and the practice in question.

361.   With respect to familiar practice, if, for example, I promised to meet someone to have a drink at five, but, on the way to keep the appointment, a serious accident occurred and it was necessary for me to convey someone immediately to an emergency care center, that could, in the absence of further complicating factors, suffice to excuse me. However, if on the way to keep the appointment it occurred to me that it would be something of a bore to keep the appointment, and that thought led me not to perform my promise, I would be morally at fault. For I was morally bound by my promise to keep the appointment. After all, I knew when I made the promise that it was

---

[42] H. A. Prichard, *Moral Obligation* (Oxford: Clarendon Press, 1949) 169.

[43] For a discussion of different conceptions of a social practice, see Stanley Cavell, *The Claim Of Reason* (Oxford: Clarendon Press, New York: Oxford University Press, 1979) 292-312. Cavell's comments and complaints about Rawls's use of the term 'practice' have no bearing on my use of that term.

likely to be a boring affair; perhaps I simply should not have made the promise. But the fact of the matter is that I did, and having made the promise, I was morally bound to keep it. That is the way it is, in so far as the familiar practice of making promises and a familiar morality is concerned.

362.   In default of a legitimate excuse, or a release from the promise, a person is morally bound to perform a promise: that does not mean that the person will perform. The bonds of morality are not unbreakable.

363.   Consider Aunt Martha's nephew after he killed her for the legacy. We could say of him that, even though he did it, he had been morally bound not to do it. Indeed, he might say to himself, "I suppose I was morally bound not to kill her -- but I needed the money." Evidently the obligation had not had sufficient force to deter him. Possibly he felt guilt or remorse, possibly not.

364.   A person may decide to break a promise while, at the same time, acknowledging that he has no legitimate excuse for doing so. The person has an obligation to keep the promise which he has decided to break. If one is to understand the force of an obligation to perform a promise, it is useless to look at, to attend to, to be concerned with that person. One must look elsewhere.

365.   There is no mystery, *pace* Prichard, about how the person came to be under the obligation. In the familiar practice of promise making, if a person makes a promise, in any of the ways in which a promise can be made, he is *ipso facto* under an obligation to perform the promise: he is morally bound to perform.

366.   But this means that the source of the obligation is to be found in the particular practice of promise making that one is concerned with. And if that is the source of the obligation, that must also be the source of the obligations power to bind one to the performance of the promise.

367.   Promise making, in one form or another, is a widespread practice. It is to be found in many different cultures.

368.   In its legal form, a promise is a contract. I am not concerned with such promises here. In so far as a contract is legally binding and legally enforceable, an obvious, and here irrelevant, source of such an obligation's power to bind one is readily found in the associated legal sanctions for nonperformance.

369.   Looking at legal promises is the wrong way to gain insight into the character of the moral obligation to keep promises. It directs one to look for covert sanctions of some sort: there are few of any significance to be found. To echo Bentham again, who always had his eyes on the law and its sanctions, "If the thunders of the law are of no avail, what can the whispers of morality achieve?"

370.   The law can shed no light on morality.

"The content of an action at law (*actio*), as something determined by legal enactment, is not imputable to me. Consequently, such an action contains only some of the moments of a moral action proper, and contains them only incidentally. The aspect of an action in virtue of which it is properly moral is therefore distinct from its aspect as legal."[44]

371.   Laws are legislated, enacted, pronounced by appropriate authorities. Some moralities have no such foundation. Certainly my morality has no such foundation.

372.   There has been, and no doubt still is, widespread misconception about this. Years ago one could hear odd types saying "God is dead: so all is permitted," the suggestion being that all moralities require an authoritarian base and, in the absence thereof cannot exist.

373.   This is not to deny that parental, familial or tribal authorities and so forth, may have a significant role to play in the etiology of a child's morality, just as they have in the etiology of a child's mathematical conceptions. But some moralities are no more based on

---

[44] Hegel, *op. cit.*, 79.

authority than is mathematics. (There are, of course, some moralities explicitly based on authorities, on texts, scriptures, the dictates of a guru and so forth: we need not be concerned with them.)

374.   Promise making is a complex social and moral practice; the details of it may well differ from culture to culture. And even within a specific culture there may be considerable variation. But children, of any culture, are not born with an understanding of what a promise is and how promises are made. Some of them acquire such an understanding in the course of their moral, social and cultural development.

375.   If a child is to acquire an understanding of the familiar practice of promise making, it will have to acquire, to form or develop, an adequate conception of commitment. I am not concerned with the etiology of the formation of such a conception: the fact of the matter is that without such a conception there can be no genuine understanding of promise making.

376.   This matter, however, is remarkably complex: it is here that the symbol minded propensities of *Homo Sapiens* are, and must be, brought into play. To make a commitment, one must have a particular conception of one's self: one must conceive of one's self as being, as it were, entrusted with something, and this conception must have symbolic efficacy. If a person is committed to a certain course of action, then the person has an image of himself or herself as performing that action: the person is then under the aegis and sway of that image.

377.   My use of the term 'image' here should not be misunderstood: I am not suggesting that what is in question is necessarily something visual. Being visual is here irrelevant. If I ask someone "Can you see yourself doing that?", the answer may be "Yes" regardless of whether the person has any sort of visual image.

378.   The child will, furthermore, have to acquire, to form or develop, an adequate conception of what it is to make a commitment to another person. For again, without that there can be no genuine understanding of promise making.

379.   Again, the matter is remarkably complex. To make a commitment to another person, one must have a conception, of the other as one who is aware of and attends to the acts or actions of the person making the commitment. Though one may greatly prize a particular tree, one cannot make a commitment to a tree; at best, one can commit oneself to performing some act or action in connection with the tree.

380.   A person making a commitment to another must have both an image of himself or herself as performing the act or action in question and an image of the other as another person: this complex image must then have efficacy; it must have sufficient power to direct and bind the person to performance. If the image lacks such efficacy then no genuine commitment has been made.

381.   The efficacy of symbols and images can hardly be exaggerated. It is absolutely essential for morality, yet it is altogether deplorable in a great variety of cases.

382.   Consider, for example, the childish feeling of embarrassment. Say a man is at home alone and his pants fall down. He would simply pull them up without feeling anything in particular, perhaps annoyance, perhaps amusement. But if his pants were to fall down in a public place, say in a classroom while giving a lecture, the average man would feel embarrassed. The reason why, of course, is that he is concerned with and attending to his own image vis-à -vis others. (When I was a child I was subject to embarrassment, but I long ago put away childish things: the only thing that could embarrass me now is being embarrassed.)

383.   Pride, one of the seven deadly sins, and rightly so accredited, is akin to embarrassment. It, too, is under the aegis and sway of imagery, the image of one's self vis-à -vis others. A person alone, and who thought himself alone, on a desert island would not, could not, feel proud of his accomplishments: he could only feel pleased with them. (There is no need for a rational being ever to suffer "the proud man's contumely".)

384.   Despite the fact that symbol minded thinking is, all too often, simple minded thinking, promising in particular, and morality in

general, requires the efficacy of symbolism and imagery. As I said previously, symbolism and imagery constitute the real and only basis of morality.

385.   A person who has acquired an understanding of the familiar practice of promise making may be reluctant to participate in that practice. Such a reluctance may be simply explicable in terms of the person's reluctance to make commitments to other persons, or perhaps, simply to make commitments. Such a reluctance might, indeed, testify to his understanding of the practice.

386.   Commitments may be strong or weak, complete or partial. If I am totally committed to performing some act or action, A, then I will, I must, perform A, or do my best to perform A, in so far as it is possible. If, however, perhaps after reflecting on the consequences of performing A, I decide not to perform A, then I could not have been totally committed to the performance of A. If one is totally committed to perform, there is then no choice to be made. Indeed, it is a *contradictio in adjecto* to say "I am totally committed to the performance of A but I have decided not to perform A".

387.   A person can become committed to something, to a course of action, to an undertaking, to another person, to a corporate entity and so forth, without ever having made an explicit commitment. But what is particularly interesting about the familiar practice of making promises is that it characteristically involves making both a commitment to another person and an explicit commitment to perform.

388.   The force and extent of a commitment is not a function of its explicitness. If two persons marry one another, in so doing each makes an explicit commitment to the other. It is possible, and the possibility is apparently being exploited more and more, to get out of such a commitment, to get a divorce. Divorces are easier to get nowadays in America than they were years ago, and this for two reasons: first, of course, the legalities have become less difficult to cope with; but secondly, and more interestingly, given the prevalence of the practice of divorce, there has been considerable erosion in the strength of the explicit commitment made in the marriage ceremony. Those married

in a wedding chapel in Reno can hardly fail to realize that the union can easily be dissolved by a quick return to Nevada and a six week sojourn; or, for the more affluent, a few days in Acapulco will accomplish the same end.

389.   In contrast, if two people simply begin to live together, without the benefit of matrimony and without any explicit commitment to one another, in time they may find that the extent and force of their mutual commitment has become so great that it is more difficult to escape than if they had, in fact, been married. (As a palliative, perhaps one should recall Paul Simon's pop hit "Fifty ways to leave a lover".)

390.   Characteristically, in making a promise to a person one makes both a commitment to that person and an explicit commitment to perform some act or other or to perform in some way or other. The familiar practice is such that, generally, one can be released from the commitment to perform by the person to whom the commitment was made. And if the promise was subject to defeasibility conditions, contingencies may provide a legitimate excuse for nonperformance. But in default of either a release or a legitimate excuse, the person is under an obligation to perform, he is morally bound to perform.

391.   The force of the obligation is to be found in the force and extent of the commitments made.

392.   Prichard said:

> "... I shall assume that on reflection we shall all have to agree that what we call 'promising' to do so and so cannot really be what the term 'promising' suggests it is. *viz.* creating an obligation to do the action, but must be the creating something else, the creation of which gives rise to the obligation to do it, and that the problem is to find out what that something is".[45]

393.   I believe that Prichard was right in that there is a question here requiring an answer. The answer is that one "creates", or better, makes

---

[45] *Op. cit.*, 170.

a commitment to a person and a commitment to perform, and it is these commitments made in the act of promising that give rise to the obligation.

394.   Prichard's own conclusion, one which he suggested "only with the greatest hesitation", was that there must have been some sort of prior agreement between persons about keeping agreements. But finding this somewhat incredible, he backed off and said:

> "... what I am suggesting is not a conclusion but rather a problem for consideration; *viz.* what is that something implied in the existence of agreements which looks very much like an agreement and yet, strictly speaking, cannot be an agreement?"[46]

395.   Prichard was, I think, in a perhaps odd way, right again. For if one person makes a commitment to another, and the other understands that such a commitment has been made, then what has happened can look very much like an agreement even though, strictly speaking, no agreement has been made.

396.   Promises are social instruments. A violin that will not play is a defective instrument. The promise made by a person who fails to perform, without either a release or a legitimate excuse, is also a defective instrument. The defect, in such a case, is a defect in the strength or the extent of the commitments made in the act of promising.

397.   Obviously, the person, who made a promise and then simply decided to ignore it, made very weak commitments; so weak that one might even say that, in such a case, the instrument was so defective as not even to constitute a promise. The person merely seemed, or pretended, to make a promise, but did not in fact do so. The person is morally at fault, but more by way of being a liar.

---

[46] *Op. cit.*, 179.

398.   More interesting problems arise when one is unsure whether or not one has a legitimate excuse to break a promise. These, of course, are problems only for those who do not construe promise making in a robot like fashion.

399.   Suppose I promise to meet someone for a tennis match but, en route to keep the appointment, I severely sprain an ankle. Having no way to contact him, I decide to return home and tell him about the problem later. Both my friends and I would accept such an excuse. After all, even if I were to hobble to the appointment, I would not be able to play; most likely, he would be able to pick up a game with someone else. Suppose, however, that I have promised to meet a person who has some emotional problem and wants someone to talk to. If en route to keep the appointment, I severely sprain an ankle, does that constitute a legitimate excuse for nonperformance? How am I to decide?

400.   I know what I would in fact consider in such a case, though I cannot say how such a process culminates in a decision. (I am inclined to think that, quite often, many people do not perform any specific act appropriately characterizable as making a decision: instead, they simply go through a process of consideration and then end up finding themselves doing one thing or another. Perhaps I am simply reporting what happens to me.)

401.   I would, as it were, compare the person's need to talk to someone with my need to tend my injured ankle. How do I do that? I don't really know. I may think: does he really have to talk to me? Perhaps I think: he wants to talk about his girl friend, they have split again for the umpteenth time. He seems to have a need to publicize the matter. Will he be in any real distress if I don't show? Perhaps he'll be satisfied to tell the bartender about his problems. But if I don't tend my ankle, I'll have to withdraw from the tennis tournament next week. And since I'm scheduled to play both singles and doubles, what will my doubles partner do? He expects us to win this tournament, a county championship, and, for him, that is important, it will effect his state ranking. It is also not unimportant to me.

402.   What would I in fact do? I don't know. If my ankle were broken, that would settle it, for I wouldn't be able to meet him. But what if it is only a severe sprain? Perhaps I say to myself, "A promise is a promise. I was stupid to make such a promise, but I did it." But I also agreed to play doubles and if I don't tend this ankle immediately, will I be able to play? If I keep the appointment and ignore my ankle, my doubles partner will consider me an idiot.

403.   What would I do? I still don't know. Even though I have described this relatively trivial situation in some detail, the description is still far too thin and sketchy for one, or at any rate for me, to attain a clear view. Should I describe the case in greater detail? Sufficient detail would be beyond both the scope of this essay and my power to describe. Here one would want to call upon the skills of Beckett or Kafka or Dostoievski. And no matter what, it would remain merely hypothetical, unreal, and I could not, I hope, delude myself into thinking otherwise. In the realm of the merely hypothetical, the satisfaction, perhaps a somewhat smug satisfaction, to be found in performing one's promise is remarkably attractive. It is not difficult to forgo the merely hypothetical chance of a championship: hypothetically limping along on an hypothetically sprained ankle en route to perform a promise doesn't hurt at all.

404.   What should one do to resolve this sort of problem? Look at the realities, of course. But when one turns to a real case, what then?

405.   When one makes a promise, how strong are the commitments that one makes? Not all commitments are equal. (Personally, I avoid making promises, in so far as I can.)

406.   At a reception for a visiting composer: "Come to our concert: we shall be performing a Brandenburg concerto; everyone will be using ancient instruments. You will be delighted!" I would not be delighted: after fifty years, I am tired both of amateur performances and of the baroque. "I will see. Perhaps I'll come." -- "Oh do come, your presence would encourage us all." -- "Yes, I see, I'll try to come." -- "Promise that you will come, please!", this said in a manner that persuades me that, after a few minutes, he will have forgotten all about the matter. He hardly knows me; I don't really know him: he sat in on

a few of my lectures on aesthetics. As far as I could tell, he understood nothing of what was said. "Do promise to come!" -- "Yes, I promise to come." On the way home, I say to myself "You are supposed to be a tough bastard: why do you give in to such pressures? Possibly I am becoming senile."

407.   So I have made a commitment, but what sort of a commitment have I made?

408.   A second case: my brother tells me that he is going to be operated on, that both his kidneys will have to be removed. He is desperately in need of a kidney transplant. I stop him at once saying "I don't need two kidneys, and you might as well use one of them. When and where is the operation to take place?" My brother: "Do you understand what is involved?" -- "Of course I do. Just remember you owe me one, but a bottle of Stolnichkaya will square everything." In each case I made a commitment, but the commitments are not comparable. If on my way to the amateur concert I sprain my ankle, I would at once return home. If on my way to the transplant operation I sprain my ankle, I would ignore it, in so far as I could, and I would continue on my way.

409.   The commitment to my brother was a strong moral commitment; my commitment to the amateur musician was a weaker commitment, so weak that I would not characterize it as a "moral commitment"; rather, I should characterize it as a "social commitment", akin to accepting an invitation to attend a reception.

410.   There is, however, something of a problem here. Is the significant difference a difference in the commitments made, or is the significant difference a difference in the gravity of the acts that I committed myself to perform?

411.   What if my brother were an amateur musician, and it was he who urged me to attend the same sort of concert? If he had said "Promise me that you will come!", I would not have thought that, after a few minutes, he would have forgotten all about the matter. In the first case, I committed myself to attending a concert at which some person that I hardly know would be performing. In the second case, I committed myself to attending a concert at which my brother would be

performing. The gravity of the act that I was committed to perform seems to be much the same in each case. So I think that there is a real difference in the commitments made to the person in each case, and not simply a difference in the gravity of the act that one commits oneself to perform.

412.   The character, the strength and extent, of the commitments made in making a promise do seem to depend on several fairly obvious factors: the seriousness, or gravity, with which the promise is made; the seriousness, or gravity, with which the promise is received and understood by the one to whom the promise is made; and the gravity of the act which the one who promises has committed himself to perform.

413.   If one so characterizes the commitments made in promising, it is not too difficult to characterize a legitimate excuse for nonperformance in terms of relative gravity. If the gravity of the reasons for nonperformance outweigh the gravity of the commitments made in the act of promising, then the reasons for nonperformance constitute a legitimate excuse for nonperformance, and if not, they do not.

414.   But how does one compare the gravity of reasons for nonperformance with the gravity of a commitment to a person and a commitment to perform?

415.   To assess and compare the gravity of reasons for the nonperformance of a promise with the gravity of the commitments made to a person and to performance one must take into account and appreciate differences between persons. However, not all differences between persons are always relevant. Furthermore, we shall need a relatively precise, although somewhat abstract, way of characterizing differences between persons with respect to values and priorities.

416.   According to Amartya Sen:

> "When Henry Sidgwick claimed that "if a kind of conduct that is right (or wrong) for me is not right (or wrong) for some one else, it must be on the ground of some difference between the two cases, other than the fact that I and he are different

persons," he used a powerful informational constraint to rule out taking note of personal identity, as such, in making these judgments of conduct."[47]

417.   On Sen's reading and with respect to a familiar morality, what Sidgwick invoked is an extreme and altogether excessive informational constraint; on another reading, one which I take to be expressive of Sidgwick's true view, what Sidgwick pronounced can, on close scrutiny, be seen to be, not "a powerful informational constraint" but, rather, a mild stricture about the insufficiency of certain grounds.

418.   Suppose I bequeath a certain volume, v, to Josef. Then on my death it would be wrong for George to claim v but not wrong for Josef. Why would it be wrong for George? Simply because v was bequeathed to Josef and he, George, is not Josef. Here the relevant difference is a difference in identity as such: a difference in the identities of the persons. (There are, of course, innumerable instances in which personal identity as such is a relevant consideration in moral matters; just think of promising: a promise to Josef is not a promise to George. Why not? Because George is not Josef.)

419.   Consider the two predicative expressions 'has been bequeathed to Josef' and 'has been bequeathed to George'. If, as Sen would have it, Sidgwick holds that appeals to personal identity as such are to be ruled out, then, for Sidgwick, there could be no relevant difference between the factors expressed by the two predicative expressions. But this would mean that Sidgwick could not claim, though certainly he would wish to claim, that it would be wrong for George to claim v but not wrong for Josef to do so.

420.   One might attempt to avoid this objection by urging that the reason it would be wrong for George to claim v is that v was bequeathed to a person named 'Josef': in the given case, however, that might simply be false. One can make a bequest to a certain person and

---

[47] Amartya Sen, "Well-being, Agency and Freedom: The Dewey Lectures 1984", *Journal of Philosophy* Vol. LXXXII, No. 4, 170-171.

not be concerned with any particular factor serving to identify that person as the proper recipient of the bequest. Thus if, unknown to me, George's real name is 'Josef', while Josef's real name is 'George', then the person whose real name is 'George', *viz.* Josef, is still the proper recipient of *v*: all that matters is the real identity of the person to whom the bequest was made, not how that person happens to be identified.

421.   If, as Sen would have it, Sidgwick did "rule out taking note of personal identity, as such," then Sidgwick did indeed impose a powerful informational constraint, but one that is, and certainly would have been deemed by Sidgwick to be, altogether excessive.

422.   There is, however, a much more plausible and relatively innocuous way of construing Sidgwick's claim. Sidgwick spoke of "some difference between the two cases other than the fact that he and I are different persons". This fact, "the fact that he and I are different persons", can be set out.

423.   Consider the differences between Josef and George with respect to personal identity. The identity of a person can be characterized in terms of a nonnull set of conditions uniquely satisfied by the person, conditions having to do with the various characteristics, properties, qualities, facts about the person and so forth such that there is an x such that x satisfies all of the conditions and for all y, if y satisfies all of the conditions then y is identical with x. Let $\{J\}$ and $\{G\}$ be such sets of conditions satisfied by Josef and George respectively. (It is inessential, and essentially irrelevant, whether these conditions be considered "essential" or not: what is relevant here are simply the differences between $\{J\}$ and $\{G\}$.) Let $\{D\}$ be the set constituted by the union of $\{J\}$ and $\{G\}$ less their intersection. $\{D\}$ then constitutes the differences between Josef and George with respect to personal identity.

424.   (For those not familiar with the set-theoretic terms "union" and "intersection" the following diagram may help to clarify matters.

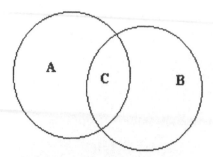

Let circle *A* be one collection, circle *B* another. The union of *A* and *B* is everything in *A* together with everything in *B*, thus *A+B*. The intersection of *A* and *B* is *C*, thus everything they have in common. The union less the intersection is simply *(A+B)-C*, thus everything in *A* that is not in *B* together with everything that is in *B* but not in *A*. A "null set" is a set having no members; e.g., the set of positive integers that are neither prime nor composite; the set of giraffes living in my garden is also a null set: alas, there are none!)

425.   The fact that Josef and George are different persons can then be expressed by saying that there is an *x* such that $\underline{x}$ satisfies all of the conditions of {*J*} and for all *z*, if *z* satisfies all of the conditions of {*J*} then *z* is identical with *x*; there is a *y* such that *y* satisfies all of the conditions of {*G*} and for all *z*, if *z* satisfies all of the conditions of {*G*} then *z* is identical with *y*; and neither {*J*} nor {*G*} nor {*D*} is identical with the null set. Or, assuming that one is concerned with persons satisfying the conditions of {*J*} and {*G*}, one could indicate that the persons are different simply by saying that {*D*} is not null, or, equivalently, there is an *x* such that *x* is a member of {*D*}.

426.   Consider the act of claiming *v*: it would be wrong for George to do it but not wrong for Josef. According to Sidgwick, there must be some difference between the two cases other than the fact that George and Josef are different persons: this is simply to say that there must be some difference other than the fact that there is an *x* such that *x* is a member of {*D*}. This in no way implies that "personal identity, as such" is to be excluded from consideration: a difference between persons is one thing, personal identity quite another. All that Sidgwick said was that a difference between persons is insufficient to establish that something is right for one but wrong for the other. But the case of

the bequest to Josef involves, not a merely a difference between persons, but a difference of persons, a difference in identity.

427.   In the case of the bequeathal of v to Josef, to say that "personal identity as such" is relevant to whether or not Josef is entitled to v is to say that some subset of the factors, $x1 \ldots xn$, such that $\{J\}=\{x1 \ldots xn\}$, is so relevant. In any given case, such a subset is, of course, bound to be a proper subset; for example, if xk is the condition that Josef's real name be 'George' but, nonetheless, Josef is entitled to v, then xk may be an irrelevant factor.

428.   Given that some person, Josef, uniquely satisfies the members of the set of conditions $\{J\}$, to exclude personal identity from consideration would be to exclude at least some proper subset of $\{J\}$ from consideration. But Sidgwick was not, in the passage cited, concerned to exclude any subset of $\{J\}$ from consideration. Sidgwick did not deny that such factors should be taken into account in moral reasoning: he was concerned to deny that the fact that there was some nonnull set $\{D\}$ was, in itself, a sufficient ground.

429.   It is, perhaps, worth stressing the fact that to deny the sufficiency of a ground is not, *ipso facto*, to exclude it from consideration. That Josef is, but George is not, entitled to v is owing to the fact Josef does, but George does not, satisfy a relevant subset of $\{J\}$. Hence one can at once infer that there is a nonnull set $\{D\}$ constituted by the union less the intersection of $\{J\}$ and $\{G\}$. If $\{D\}$ were not nonnull, then George would indeed be entitled to v, for if $\{D\}$ were null, George and Josef would be one and the same person. Hence, in this particular case, that $\{D\}$ is nonnull is a relevant consideration.

430.   Sidgwick's claim, so construed, is then merely a mild stricture to the effect that mere differences between persons are insufficient grounds. Such a stricture can hardly be considered to be an informational constraint.[48]

---

[48] I am indebted to Professor Sen for comments on an earlier version of this discussion.

431.   That people differ in their priorities and values is a matter that one must appreciate in any study of morality. We each differ in our attitudes, wants, needs, inclinations, desires and so forth. Of course, there are many shared needs, wants and so forth. We all need food, water and air and many other things. But priority and value differences between persons are impressive in moral matters. When priorities and values are different, the differences can result in a moral conflict.

432.   Let $\{Pi\}$ and $\{Pj\}$ be sets of characteristics serving to determine the personal identity of persons Pi and Pj, respectively. Let the set $\{D\}$ be the union less the intersection of the sets $\{Pi\}$ and $\{Pj\}$; $\{D\}$ then serves to characterize the difference between the two persons: it constitutes a set of personal variance factors that may be in play, and, if so, must then be taken into account, in any moral conflict between the two persons.

433.   The clearest cases in which personal variance factors are in play are those that call for attention to ends rather than means.

434.   A trip to the dentist is, for many of us, of value only as a means, the end being relief from pain, or the prevention of dental caries and so forth. In contrast, a run on a beach along the water's edge is, for some of us, of value both as a means, to the end of an improved cardio-vascular condition, and as an end in itself. Some of us run on a beach simply for the sake of running on a beach: for some of us, it is a delightful thing to do. But others view such an activity, to quote Henry Aiken, "with mixed feelings: a mixture, that is, of loathing, nausea and disgust".[49]

435.   Owing to personal variance factors, what is deemed of value or disvalue by one person may not be deemed of value or disvalue by another. And owing to personal variance factors, the priorities of one person need not be, and often are not, congruent with those of another.

436.   Running on a beach is deemed of value by some, not by others. Is it of value? Can one who judges it to be of value be in error?

---

[49] I am much indebted to Henry Aiken for years of delightful and stimulating philosophic discussion.

437.   Here one must distinguish between what is called "intrinsic value" and "extrinsic value". Something is of extrinsic value if it is of value as a means to some end. Something is of intrinsic value if it is an end in itself.

438.   Whether or not running on a beach is extrinsically valuable is certainly open to question. Running on a beach may be conducive to tendonitis of the knees. Assuming that having tendonitis is not a goal to be sought after, and, indeed, that it is something to be avoided, at least one extrinsically disvaluable feature of running on a beach is then immediately discernible. But running on a beach is also conducive to an improved cardio-vascular condition. In so far as having an improved cardio-vascular condition is a goal for some, for some that constitutes an extrinsically valuable feature of running on a beach.

439.   Questions of extrinsic value are evidently amenable to rational consideration. One has merely to determine what ends are in question and then assess the utility of the means for accomplishing such ends. But this is not to say that one can always easily arrive at a final assessment of extrinsic value: personal priorities may then come into consideration.

440.   Some elect to go running on a beach knowing full well both that such a practice tends to improve one's cardio-vascular condition and that such a practice is conducive to tendonitis of the knees and other ailments that runners are particularly susceptible to. There is a trade off between the disvalue of tendonitis and the value of an improved cardio-vascular condition. For some, the cardio-vascular improvement wins out; for others, the possibility of tendonitis is an effective deterrent.

441.   But are questions of intrinsic value similarly open to rational assessment? Is running on a beach of intrinsic value? Can one who deems running on a beach to be of intrinsic value, to be an end in itself, be in error?

442.   To say that running on a beach is intrinsically valuable could be to say, at least, either or both of two quite different things. If George says that running on a beach is intrinsically valuable, he might be saying simply that, for him, running on a beach is an end in itself;

or he might be saying that, for everyone, it is, or should be, an end in itself. Here and now, I am concerned only with the first claim: if it is open to rational assessment then so is the second.

443.   Bentham somewhere said: "Prejudice apart, the game of push-pin is of equal value with the arts and sciences of music and poetry", and Mill replied: "Who would not rather be Socrates dissatisfied than a pig satisfied?". Mill never put the question to a pig.

444.   By "prejudice", of course, Bentham meant prior interests; and in his reference to a pig, Mill was concerned to point out that there is a natural delimitation to the field of inquiry imposed by the innate characteristics of *Homo Sapiens*. Both, in a way, were right, but, more importantly, both were wrong.

445.   Bentham was right in that one cannot ignore personal variance factors in estimates of value. And Mill was right in insisting that personal variance factors are constrained by innate limits. But Mill was quite mistaken in supposing that innate factors could serve to resolve the difficulties that Bentham was pointing to. And Bentham was wrong in supposing that prior interests are not amenable to rational assessment and evaluation.

446.   The interests of persons are enormously varied; the ends persons seek or strive after do not admit of any simple cataloging. Furthermore, they are subject to change throughout a person's life. Nonetheless, if one approaches the matter somewhat abstractly, one can characterize the intrinsic values of a person, Pi, at some moment of time, in terms of an ordered set of intrinsic values, $\{Vpi\}$, where the ordering reflects Pi's priority rankings at that time. The term "values" is here to be understood broadly and loosely as a portmanteau term for such diverse matters as ends, aims, goals, for whatever is prized, wanted, sought after and so forth. Thus for a given individual, Pa, in America, $\{Vpa\}$ might include such matters as making money, doing well at his or her job, playing golf, solving business problems, jogging, making love, raising children, getting high on cocaine, gaining power over others, being a good parent, being a good citizen, smoking, drinking fine wines, playing with guns and so forth. Thus all the things, no matter what, that the particular person finds being and

doing worthwhile for their own sake, as ends and not merely as means. (If one wished to be more precise here, a set of such values, $\{Vpi\}$, could be assigned a temporal index, for $\{Vpi\}$ at one time is not likely to be identical with $\{Vpi\}$ at a much later time. But I shall not bother.)

447.   The set $\{Vpi\}$ is an ordered set, where the ordering reflects Pi's priority rankings. Where vi and vj are members of $\{Vpi\}$ ($i<>j$), to say that vi has a higher priority ranking than vj is to say, not that Pi deems vi to be of greater value than vj, but that Pi is more concerned to achieve or to realize the value of vi than vj. Thus although I deem both drinking a martini and attempting to understand a philosophic problem to be of intrinsic value, the latter has, for me, the higher priority ranking. And although I would consider the possession of a Lamborghini Countach to be of greater intrinsic value than the drinking of a martini, since I am not seriously prepared to do anything to acquire a Lamborghini but I am, on occasion, prepared to do what is required to obtain a martini, for me, the drinking of a martini has a higher priority rating than the possession of a Lamborghini. It should be clear that priorities and preferences have little connection: given the choice, I would prefer owning and driving a Lamborghini Countach to drinking a martini.

448.   A particular intrinsic value, vi, a member of $\{Vpi\}$, is open to rational assessment both in virtue of its membership in $\{Vpi\}$ and in virtue of Pi's position in his ecosystem. The set $\{Vpi\}$, given a priority ranking of the members of the set, can be rationally evaluated in terms of fitness, completeness and compatibility.

449.   An instance of unfitness is to be found in the case of $P1$, an elderly person of extremely limited means, one who lives at or below a poverty level, but who, nonetheless, is obsessed with the acquisition of a Lamborghini Countach. He is not, however, prepared to obtain the car by dishonest means. Given $P1$'s position in his ecosystem, the acquisition of a Lamborghini is a virtual impossibility.

450.   There is, of course, a tradition for this sort of unfitness: "Dream the impossible dream!", "Aim at the stars!", "One shouldn't set one's sights too low!" and so forth. No doubt one should not forget the power of positive thinking. But, on the other hand, there is a fine

line here that a rational being cannot transgress: a rational being has to have some grip on reality.

451.   "One shouldn't set one's sights too low!" has the rational corollary: "One shouldn't set one's sights too high!". The impossible dream may have a deleterious effect on one's other dreams. To cultivate tastes that are impossible to satisfy is to invite perpetual frustration. More generally, if vi is a member of $\{Vpi\}$, vi is virtually impossible to achieve and vi has a high priority ranking, the achievement of vj $(i<>j)$ is likely to be both delayed, owing to the expenditure of effort in pursuit of vi, and of less significance for Pi than it would otherwise have had were it not for the inclusion of vi in $\{Vpi\}$.

452.   It is important to note that the unfitness of $\{Vp1\}$ is not attributable simply to the fact that vi is a member of $\{Vp1\}$, but, rather, is primarily owing to the fact that vi is here being assumed to have a high priority ranking. This is to say that, for $P1$, not only is the possession of a Lamborghini Countach deemed to be of intrinsic value, but it is an end that $P1$ is much concerned to achieve. Thus, instead of using what funds he has available in a rational manner, his lust for a Lamborghini may drive him to purchase large and expensive numbers of state lottery tickets and the like.

453.   Completeness is a more complicated matter. Consider a person, $P2$, who has few interests in life. He is a middle aged blue-collar worker in a textile factory. After work, he goes home to a small drab house and an apathetic silent middle aged wife. He enjoys a beer before dinner and then, after dinner, another two beers while watching the television. He can but he doesn't read or write anything. He has no hobbies, he plays no sports. On weekends he sleeps late and then, in the afternoon and evening, watches television. He and his wife are childless. They have few friends whom they hardly ever see.

454.   If one considers the set of $P2$'s intrinsic values, the set $\{Vp2\}$, one can't help but be struck by the paucity of its membership. But paucity is a relative notion. What is $\{Vp2\}$ being compared with?

455.   There are, at least, two possible candidates here. Let Pr be some ideal person. Then, possibly, in complaining of the paucity of

membership of $\{Vp2\}$, one can be conceived of as comparing $\{Vp2\}$ with $\{Vpr\}$, the set of intrinsic values of Pr. Perhaps from the viewpoint of Pr, $\{Vp2\}$ would be seen as a poverty stricken version of $\{Vpr\}$.

456.   But whose ideals are in question, and why should they be invoked in a rational assessment of $\{Vp2\}$? The trouble with "impersonal" ideals is that, when looked at with a neutral critical eye, they inevitably prove to be personal, parochial or paternalistic.

457.   Rather than invoking parochial ideals, one should reflect on Mill's pig. I don't know whether a pig can be satisfied, but a pig can have a good or a bad life. A pig has wants and needs and these wants and needs may be met. It is reported that Robert Herrick would prop up a pig in a chair and read his poetry to the pig. That the pig did not, could not, appreciate "Whenas in silks my Julia goes" would not be a criticism of the pig: one expects only piggish things of pigs.

458.   As a person, $P2$ has various capacities and potentialities. Given $P2$'s capacities and potentialities, and given $P2$'s particular position in his ecosystem, one can form a conception of a set of values, $\{Vp2'\}$, of an hypothetical person, $P2'$, who constitutes, as it were, an enhanced version of $P2$, one who has realized $P2$'s potentialities and who has availed himself of the opportunities provided in his ecosystem. Relative to $\{Vp2'\}$, $\{Vp2\}$ can then be seen to be a distinctly incomplete set.

459.   Consider a young parent, $P3$, who adores his young children, who finds being a good parent intrinsically valuable, but who is also a sports car enthusiast and finds driving on local highways at great speed, in excess of 100 miles an hour, also to be something intrinsically valuable.

460.   It seems reasonable to believe that $P3$'s set of values, $\{Vp3\}$, is somewhat incoherent in virtue of compatibility considerations. High speed driving on local highways is conducive to either an immanent demise, or hospitalization owing to injuries or incarceration in a local jail owing to a traffic violation; but being a good parent requires one to survive, to be relatively intact and to be at liberty, at least until the children are mature enough to be on their own. Of course, $P3$'s priority

rankings must be taken into account. But unless high speed driving on local highways has the highest priority for *P3*, one can readily conclude that {*Vp3*} is somewhat incoherent. And this is to say that *P3*'s set of intrinsic values is not altogether rational.

461.   Incompatibility of values is not an uncommon occurrence. One who finds smoking valuable but who is also concerned to cultivate his appreciation of fine wines is at odds with himself. That smoking dulls one's olfactory sensibility may be one of its virtues in modern society, but it seriously interferes with wine tasting: one can hardly test the nose of a wine if one's own nose is filled with smoke.

462.   To evaluate a set of intrinsic values, {*Vpi*}, solely on the basis of considerations of fitness, completeness and compatibility is to attend exclusively to personal features, features that are peculiar to the person in question. (It should, however, be noted that we have established part of the main thesis of this essay, *viz*, that with respect to the various values and priorities that different people have, some are open to criticism on rational grounds; others, no doubt, are not open to such criticism.)

463.   But is it also possible rationally to evaluate an intrinsic value or a set of intrinsic values from an impersonal viewpoint? This is a complex problem that can only be approached circumspectly.

464.   Renford Bambrough has offered a "proof" that we have moral knowledge:

> "My proof that we have moral knowledge consists in essentially saying, "We know that this child, who is about to undergo what would otherwise be painful surgery, should be given an anesthetic before the operation. Therefore we know at least one moral proposition to be true." I argue that no proposition that could plausibly be alleged as a reason in favor of doubting the truth of the proposition that the child should be

given an anesthetic can possibly be more certainly true than that proposition itself."[50]

465.   What is interesting about this alleged "proof" is its implication: if the proposition in question were, in fact, a rationally undeniable truth, then it would also be a rationally undeniable truth that a child's pain is intrinsically disvaluable. That would be an interesting truth, if it were a truth, but it isn't.

466.   This alleged "proof" fails in two ways. First, it requires patching if it is to be even plausible. But secondly, and more importantly, it simply ignores personal variance factors that can serve to skew the relevant priorities and value judgments of the persons concerned.

467.   There was a child who was about to undergo surgery. He was suffering from a severe case of pneumonia; he also had severely abscessed ears. The doctors deemed it essential that the abscesses in both ears be lanced immediately. The condition of the child's lungs was such that the doctors did not dare risk a general anesthesia. There was then, however, no means of administering a local anesthetic. (This case is real: the surgery was performed successfully, but it was excruciatingly painful to the child. Owing to advances in anesthesiology, an appropriate anesthetic would today pose no problems.) Perhaps it is merely the example that is unfortunate. Can it be patched up?

468.   "A child who is about to undergo what would otherwise be painful surgery, and to whom an anesthetic can safely be administered without any ill effects or harmful consequences, should be given an anesthetic before the operation." Is it true that there is no proposition that could plausibly be alleged as a reason in favor of doubting the truth of this proposition that can possibly be more certainly true than this proposition itself? Possibly there is such a proposition. Possibly

---

[50] Renford Bambrough, "A Proof of the Objectivity of Morals", *The American Journal of Jurisprudence* 1969: 45-46.

what is wanted here, however, is an expertise that I lack. But one can conjecture.

469.   From a neurophysiological point of view, pain is associated with the stimulation of certain fibers, or so I have been told. It is conceivable that the stimulation of such fibers could be requisite for an alteration of neurophysiological structures that would prove beneficial to the patient. Thus conceive of a case in which the child is subject to an esoteric type of seizure, and the received, and well established, medical opinion is that the physiological correlates of an experience of pain would prove beneficial to the child, would cure the child of such seizures. Does this strain one's powers of conception? I think not. But if all this were so, the truth of the proposition in question would be in question. In such a case, perhaps one could claim that the experience of pain was, at least, extrinsically valuable. Perhaps not. (There can be no doubt, however, that for some, an experience of pain is extrinsically valuable: some American Indian tribes required an ordeal of pain as a proof of one's manhood.) Perhaps another patch is wanted.

470.   "Given the present state of the medical arts, and of psychological and neurophysiological knowledge, all of which indicate that there are no medical benefits to be derived from the experience of pain that outweigh the negative value of pain, a child who is about to undergo what would otherwise be painful surgery, and to whom an anesthetic can safely be administered without any ill effects or harmful consequences, should be given an anesthetic before the operation." I think I am inclined to agree with this proposition, but I do not know what it can prove: knowledge and the state of an art changes daily, and not all benefits are medical benefits. And what warrants the assumption that pain has a negative value? As far as I am concerned, that is true, but there are others who think otherwise.

471.   More precisely, there are moralities according to which an experience of pain is valuable. Think of Luther:

> "It is reported that Luther, when someone proposed Glucklichkeit (happiness) as the end of human life, violently

rejected the idea and said "leiden, leiden, Kreuz, Kreuz" ("suffering ... the cross ...")."[51]

472.   And then think of the Jains, of Maha-vira and his followers, who practiced asceticism and self mortification. Possibly such persons deemed an experience of pain to be, not merely extrinsically, but intrinsically valuable. Furthermore, there do seem to be people who actually enjoy pain, for example, masochists who take delight in being abused by their sexual partners.

473.   I do not think there is any warrant for the unqualified claim that pain, or anything else, is either intrinsically disvaluable or intrinsically valuable. In this respect, I agree with Bentham: what is or is not of intrinsic value, or of intrinsic disvalue, wholly depends on the person. Intrinsic values are subject to rational evaluation only in terms of a priority ordered set of values relative to a particular person.

474.   Given a morality in which principles and obligations are subject to defeasibility conditions, there may be legitimate excuses for the nonperformance of a promise. In a familiar morality, to determine whether or not a given excuse is a legitimate excuse one may have to assess and compare the gravity of reasons for the nonperformance of the promise with the gravity of the commitments made to a person and to performance. But, owing to the operation of personal variance factors, this can be remarkably difficult to do: one must appreciate and have some insight into the priorities and values of the persons concerned.

475.   In attempting to determine whether or not a person, Pi, has a legitimate excuse for nonperformance, one has first to attend to, and attempt to form some conception of, Pi's own priorities and values. Let $\{Vpi\}$ be the ordered set of Pi's intrinsic values, where the ordering is determined by Pi's own priority rankings. It is essential to realize that some fact that may be accredited a legitimate excuse for one person, need not be similarly accredited for another. If the fact in

---

[51] Bernard Williams, *Morality: An Introduction To Ethics* (London: Harper & Row Publishers, 1972) 82.

question constitutes the realization of some value, vi, then Pi may have a legitimate excuse for nonperformance even though Pj does not; for vi may have a very high priority ranking in $\{Vpi\}$, but a very low ranking in $\{Vpj\}$.

476.   Thus suppose that $P4$ has promised to meet someone to discuss certain problems in biology but, en route, $P4$ espies a butterfly which he then sets off in pursuit of. In consequence, he fails to perform his promise. Suppose the same thing happens with $P5$. $P4$ may have a legitimate excuse for nonperformance while $P5$ does not. For suppose that $P4$ is a passionate butterfly collector; the butterfly he espied was of an absolutely unknown type and its acquisition would be of enormous intrinsic value to $P4$. On the other hand, $P5$ is an arachnologist and has but a slight interest in butterflies; on this occasion, however, he was somewhat intrigued and simply wandered off in pursuit: it was of no genuine importance to him whether he actually collected it or not. One would, in consequence, assign a slight weight to the gravity of his reason for nonperformance, while assigning considerably greater weight to the gravity of $P4$'s reason for nonperformance.

477.   Secondly, one must attempt to arrive at a rational assessment of $\{Vpi\}$. The set $\{Vpi\}$ may, to begin with, be assessed solely in terms relative to the person, thus in terms of fitness, completeness and compatibility.

478.   If $\{Vpi\}$ is judged to be unfit, or radically incomplete or incoherent in virtue of compatibility considerations, and if the reasons for the nonperformance of a promise are attributable to those features of $\{Vpi\}$ in virtue of which it is unfit, or radically incomplete or incoherent, then to that extent one assigns a slighter weight to the reasons for nonperformance.

479.   Thus if Pi is $P1$, the poverty stricken type obsessed with acquiring a Lamborghini Countach, and his reason for the nonperformance of a promise was that, feeling lucky, he had to buy some lottery tickets at once, the purchase of which necessitated nonperformance, one would, in consequence, assign a slight weight to the gravity of his reason for nonperformance.

480.   Unfortunately, although the conception of a priority ordered set of values can serve to direct and focus one's attention, when it comes to actual cases matters are often so complex as to preclude the possibility of any easy judgment.

481.   Reginald, who has the appropriate blood type, has promised to be a donor for his friend, Arthur, who is to undergo an operation. The operation is scheduled for 8:00 a.m. the next morning; both the staff and the patient are ready. Arthur will be psychologically distressed if the operation is delayed. Just before leaving for the hospital at 6:00 a.m. the next morning, Reginald, who is a journalist, learns that he has been assigned to cover a terrorist incident then in process in Beirut: he must leave on the 7:00 a.m. flight if he is to cover the story. He decides to call off the donation and, instead, catches the 7:00 a.m. flight for Beirut.

482.   Did Reginald have a legitimate excuse for nonperformance? Did the gravity of the reasons for nonperformance outweigh the gravity of the commitments made in the act of promising?

483.   What were Reginald's reasons for nonperformance? The donation of blood would have required him to forgo the assignment, for I am supposing that considerable blood would have been required and that, in consequence, Reginald would have been somewhat debilitated for at least a few days. Furthermore, the donation would have constituted something of a psychological trauma for Reginald, from which it would have taken him some time to recover. By the time that he had recovered, there would have been no newsworthy incident to report. And anyway, someone else would have been assigned to the story. Reginald also believed, rightly, that another donor could be found without difficulty.

484.   The reasons for performance seem clear enough: he had made a commitment to Arthur; he had committed himself to performance; without Reginald's donation, the operation had to be delayed until another donor was found; as could have been foreseen, his friend, Arthur, had been somewhat distressed.

485.   Did Reginald have a legitimate excuse for nonperformance?

486.   Reginald thinks he did: Arthur thinks not. Reginald is not a totally self-serving person, he is not blatantly immoral, but Arthur thinks Reginald made the wrong decision; at the very least, he should have delayed his departure until another donor was found. Arthur thinks that Reginald was morally at fault. Some of his other friends agree with him. Some of Reginald's colleagues, however, agree with him. Who is right?

487.   Either Reginald was morally at fault or he wasn't. How can one decide?

488.   It should be clear that there can be no easy resolution here. It is true that a promise was made, but it is also true that there can be legitimate excuses for nonperformance. To resolve the issue calls for a comparison of the gravity of the reasons for the nonperformance of the promise with the gravity of the commitments made to the person and to performance; but how is that to be done?

489.   How important was the assignment for Reginald? And here importance can have many different facets. Was it an assignment he had been waiting for for years? Was it is his first opportunity to cover an important story? Was it a once in a life-time career opportunity? Did he have someone, perhaps a lover, waiting for him in Beirut? How difficult a decision was it for Reginald to decide to go to Beirut rather than perform his promise? How serious are the commitments that Reginald makes?

490.   The unfortunate fact of the matter is that, when one tries to decide whether or not another person is morally at fault, one is all too likely to find oneself wallowing in an epistemological morass.

491.   Despite epistemological difficulties, one is often faced with the necessity of forming some judgment. Thus if one interacts socially with Reginald, one will take up some attitude or other towards his behavior: one is likely to be more or less coerced by circumstances. If Reginald asks "Do you think I was wrong?", one has to come up with an answer, or at least a response of some kind. Even if one replies "I simply don't know", one is expressing a judgment of a sort, or at least adopting a particular moral stance, for, in so saying, one is indicating that there is doubt about the rectitude of Reginald's behavior.

492.   And from this standpoint one can see that, for some moralities, there can be no unresolvable moral dilemmas. By this, I do not mean that, for some, there cannot be genuine moral problems, nor that some cannot feel themselves at a loss to decide which way to turn. But, with respect to some moralities, one is morally required to arrive at a moral decision. (For a somewhat similar point:

> "... although dilemmas are not settled without residue, the recognition of their reality has a dynamic force. It motivates us to arrange our lives and institutions with a view to avoiding such conflicts. It is the underpinning for a second-order regulative principle: that as rational agents with some control of our lives and institutions, we ought to conduct our lives and arrange our institutions so as to minimize predicaments of moral conflict."[52])

493.   In some moralities, in default of any better means, one simply cuts the Gordian knot.

494.   Suppose there were a local town council vote to determine whether or not to institute a local campaign in support of a ban on abortion, and suppose that a member of the council felt at a loss how to vote. The chairman of the council, realizing that some members might be reluctant to vote, has instituted the rule that abstentions are to be counted as negative votes. Circumstances would then force the members to do one of three things: cast an affirmative vote, cast a negative vote or resign from the council. But to resign would be to abnegate one's position in the community; it would be to shirk one's moral and civic responsibilities. One would then be forced to cast either an affirmative or, in effect, a negative vote.

495.   Some moral agents confronted with a moral problem are like members of such a council.

496.   Consider a seemingly simple case: George and Josef's proposed trip to the beach together. George and Josef are good friends,

---

[52] Ruth Barcan Marcus, *op. cit.*, 121.

they live together. Josef despises exercise but enjoys basking in the sun. George wants to run along the water's edge: sun-bathing is of no concern to him. The weather forecast for the beach is uncertain; there is a possibility of rain. George thinks they should go. Josef thinks not. The rain would make no difference to George, all the difference to Josef. Both agree that the trip, in itself, is something of a drag. This simple situation could easily escalate to a minor but intricate moral problem.

497.   George and Josef live together in an isolated rural farm house. They jointly own and share one car. This is their last free weekend for the season. George wants to go to the beach. Josef doesn't. If George is to go to the beach alone, Josef will have to agree to George's taking the car. But if George goes alone, that will leave Josef stranded at home without transportation. George says "Let's go to the beach." Josef says "No." So there is a problem. What ought they to do?

498.   Of course this is a minor matter, but it is the stuff that a great deal of life is made of. And here one can see clearly, in this simple matter, the futility of so-called "self-interest" theories of morality.

499.   What will further Josef's self-interest? If he goes to the beach and it is raining, he will suffer both the trip and boredom at the beach. If George goes without him, he will be stranded at home. So Josef's conclusion may seem clear: for Josef, self-interest dictates that they both stay home. Possibly there are persons for whom such a line of thought would suffice to resolve the issue. But this line of reasoning cannot be attributed to Josef given the assumption that George and Josef are good friends.

500.   An appeal to self-interest is idle, accomplishes nothing, if one's interests include an interest in the well-being of others.

501.   There are games that ethicists and economists are prone to play here: any interest of a person, of, as it were, "a self", is taken by definition to be a "self-interest"; hence everyone is moved by self-interest, and self-interest alone. But this game is not worth playing.

502.   (Amartya Sen has provided a concise analysis of such definitional foolery in the realm of economics:

"The reduction of man to a self-seeking animal depends in this approach on careful definition. If you are observed to choose x rejecting y, you are declared to have "revealed" a preference for x over y. Your personal utility is then defined as simply a numerical representation of this "preference", assigning a higher utility to a "preferred" alternative. With this set of definitions you can hardly escape maximizing your own utility, except through inconsistency. ... But if you are consistent, then no matter whether you are a single-minded egoist or a raving altruist or a class conscious militant, you will appear to be maximizing your own utility in this enchanted world of definitions."[53])

503.   Josef thinks: if I go and it is raining at the beach, I will suffer both the trip and boredom at the beach. If I don't go and George stays home because of me, then he will be deprived of his last chance to run on the beach this season. If I don't go and George goes anyway, then his time at the beach may be spoiled because of guilt feelings about me being left stranded at home. I guess I ought to go.

504.   George thinks: this is my last chance to run on the beach this season, but if we both go and it rains, Josef will have a miserable time. If I go alone and Josef is left stranded, he will have a miserable time. I guess I ought to forget it.

505.   What each might try is to imagine himself in the other's position.

506.   So George thinks: if I were Josef, I guess I would decide to go to the beach. It's true that it may prove to be a drag, but I wouldn't have to feel guilty about depriving me, George, of a run on the beach. Josef knows how much that means to me. Anyway, it might not rain. I think we ought to go.

507.   And Josef thinks: if I were George, would I decide not to go? That would mean I'd lose my last chance to run on a beach this season.

---

[53] Amartya Sen, "Rational Fools: A Critique of the Behavioral Foundations of Economic Theory", *Philosophy and Public Affairs*, Summer 1977, Vol. 6, No. 4. Cf. 322-323.

Of course, I'd then feel guilty about stranding me, Josef, at home. On the other hand, if I were George, I would really feel deprived if this last chance of a visit to the beach were missed because of me, Josef. And what the hell, it might not rain. I guess we ought to go.

508.   So they decide to go together to the beach. If the sun shines, all will go well. But if it rains, George will feel guilty even though he may still enjoy his run, and Josef will be bored, but he may also feel somewhat virtuous at his self-sacrifice. So each will benefit if the sun shines but each will suffer a bit if it rains.

509.   What makes the matter so complicated is the intrusion of unknown factors. How likely is it to rain? How important is running on the beach to George? Which is worse for Josef: being bored at the beach or being stranded alone at home? Will being stranded alone at home throw him into a deep depression? Does Josef enjoy taking chances? Are they optimistic types? How guilty will George feel if he leaves Josef alone at home? How guilty will he feel if Josef comes to the beach and it rains? What effect would different judgments have on their friendship?

510.   George and Josef have a friend Sidney. Sidney is something of a pessimistic recluse. Sidney tells them that George ought to go to the beach alone, that Josef ought to stay home. Sidney says "If I were you Josef, I'd stay home: self-sacrifice would be no source of satisfaction to me, and being stranded at home alone wouldn't bother me at all." But, of course, if he had Josef's character, maybe it would. And he says to George "If I were you George, I wouldn't feel guilty about Josef being home alone." But, again, if he had George's character, maybe he would.

511.   Sidney, judging the matter from his position, has arrived at one judgment; George and Josef, judging the matter from their own positions, and in terms of their own personal involvement, have arrived at a different judgment.

512.   Does this mean that moral judgments are what Amartya Sen has called "position-relative"? Sen has argued in support of what he calls "position-relativity" and "authorship invariance", where the latter

conception is invoked to allow for the "objectivity" of moral valuations. I propose to consider his argument in some detail.

513.

> "If some act - such as knifing a friend - is a bad thing to do and if the agent who did the knifing was responsible for that act, then that special badness must be a part of the over-all evaluation, made by the knifer, of that state."

Why must it be a part of the over-all evaluation made by the knifer? Surely, that depends on the knifer, on what sort of person he is, his morality, his character and so forth. I believe, but perhaps the knifer doesn't believe, that knifing a friend is a bad thing to do: if he doesn't then that special badness will not be a part of his over-all evaluation. Furthermore, even if the knifer does think it a bad thing to knife a friend, why "must" he take that into account in his over-all evaluation of the state? He should take it into account. If he is a rational moral person then perhaps he would take it into account. There is no necessity here.

514.   (Cont.)

> " It could, of course, still be the case that, despite the badness of that action, everything considered, knifing Caesar produced a better state of affairs even from the evaluative position of Brutus ("Not that I loved Caesar less, but that I loved Rome more"). However, Brutus cannot evaluate the state, of which his killing Caesar is a part, without taking note of his own responsibility for that act."

Since Brutus (assuming Brutus to be the character depicted in the Shakespearean play) was a rational moral person, he would take note of his own responsibility for the act. This, however, is simply a fact about that Brutus. But one can readily conceive of another Brutus, one so appalled by his act that he blots it out of his mind completely: accordingly, in his over-all, evaluation of the state, his own agency is not taken into account.

515.   (Cont.)

> "A consistent moral approach may, therefore, require that the moral valuation function be position-relative. Given Brutus's role in the knifing of Caesar, Brutus cannot view the resulting state - of which that knifing was also a part - in the same way as, say, Appian, the historian, completely uninvolved in the matter, can."[54]

The claim that Brutus "cannot view" the resulting state in the same way as Appian certainly seems excessive and unwarranted. Whether he could or could not view it in one way or another would depend on his capacity to adopt an impersonal perspective on the situation. Many persons have such a capacity, but, of course, many do not. I am inclined to think that Shakespeare's Brutus had, or could have had, such a capacity.

516.   (Cont.)

> "The difference can exist even when Appian and Brutus share exactly the same moral approach, and it arises because of the objective differences in their position vis-à-vis the state in question. A position-relative valuation function builds in the parameter of the assessor's position within the valuation function itself (Footnote to Sen's paper). Consider the following imaginary remark of Appian to Brutus: "If I were you, Brutus, I should have evaluated the state to be even worse than I do now, not having been involved in the knifing of Caesar myself." The statement is of the form $f(x,a,b){<}f(x,a,a)$, in which $f(x,a,b)$ is the valuation of the state x by a (Appian) in the position of b (Brutus), and $f(x,a,a)$ the valuation made by Appian from his own position."

That Appian's over-all valuation of the state be either better than, or worse than or equal to Brutus's own valuation depends on particular

---

[54] Amartya Sen, "Well-being, Agency and Freedom: The Dewey Lectures 1984", *Journal of Philosophy* Vol. LXXXII, No. 4, 170-171.

assumptions (or, if you like, facts) about Brutus and Appian. Perhaps Appian deems knifing a friend to be an absolutely horrific act, whereas Brutus deems it to be merely bad. That Appian and Brutus "share exactly the same moral approach" does not preclude the possibility of their valuations of an act differing in degree. Thus one can imagine Appian saying "If I were you, Brutus, I should have evaluated the state to be better than I do now, given that you don't share my horror about knifing a friend." If one is to speak of "the valuation made by Appian from his own position", one has to take into account precisely what Appian's position is supposed to be. If talk about "position" is to make any sense in moral matters, it is not sufficient to consider simply the physical position of a person; for example, consider two prisoners locked in the same cell: are they in the same position? In a trivial sense they are, but their actual positions may be radically different: one has wrongly, the other, rightly, been incarcerated. Nor is it sufficient to consider only the act or actions a person performs, or has performed. One must also take into account the person's moral stance, character, sensitivity, the person's capacities and abilities, for example, the person's capacity to empathize with others, to appreciate and imaginatively enter into another's position and so forth.

517.   (Cont.)

> "Notice that the relativity in question links not to the authorship (the second variable), but to the position from which the evaluation is being made (the third variable), i.e. whether a's position or b's. The authorship is immaterial for "position relativity" of a moral system."

> "Indeed, that the approach is not subject-relative (and does not include "subjectivism" within the system) can be guaranteed by insisting on an invariance requirement regarding authorship. "Authorship invariance" requires that the moral valuations of a state in a given moral system must not vary with the person making the judgment, even though it can vary with the position from which the valuation is to be made. Despite Appian's assertion (stated earlier) that $f(x,a,b) < f(x,a,a)$, which shows position-relativity, Appian would be bound by the requirements of authorship invariance to assert

f(x,a,b)=f(x,b,b).(Footnote) "You, Brutus, should evaluate the
state in the same unfavorable way as I should if I were in your
position."''

"The possibility of combining position relativity with
authorship invariance is also the reason why positionality of
moral valuation is perfectly consistent with objectivity of
moral values. Moral valuation can be position-relative in the
same way as such statements as "The sun is setting." The truth
of that statement varies with the position of the person, but it
cannot vary from person to person among those standing in the
same position."[55]

It must be noted that the requirement that moral valuation "cannot vary
from person to person among those standing in the same position" is
wholly vacuous: owing to personal variance factors, no two persons
ever are in the same position with respect to moral valuations. A
person may attempt imaginatively to enter into and appreciate another
person's position, but to imagine oneself being in a certain position is
not to be in that position.

518.   Owing to personal variance, there is no reason to expect the
moral evaluations of different persons to be absolutely congruent in all
respects.

519.   The notions of being "position-relative" and of "authorship
invariance" are both somewhat misconceived: the roles they are
devised to play are better performed by the notion of personal variance
factors. To put it somewhat cryptically, position-relative is too
relative, while authorship invariance is too invariant.

520.   There is a serious error here that arises from an unfortunate and
unrealistic methodological stance. Authorship invariance is a
reasonable requirement only if one views matters synchronically. But a
commitment to synchronism is an error that has vitiated a great deal of
both scientific and philosophic research. All human concerns are

---

[55] Amartya Sen, *loc. cit.*, 184.

subject to a diachronic evolution. Owing to the operation of personal variance factors, authorship invariance can be no more than an ideal that one approaches perhaps only asymptotically. The demands of objectivity nowhere require absolute and immediate authorship invariance: there is no rational warrant for attempting to impose such a restriction on moral valuations. What is required, or at any rate, wanted, is a diachronically realizable convergence of disparate valuations.

521.   For example, if two medical doctors give different prognoses, one does not at once level a charge of subjectivism. On the contrary, one then calls for a conference, an exchange of views, opinions, a joint examination of relevant data and so forth. Astrophysical matters are no different. There is, today, a remarkable difference of opinion about the nature of quasars: one hopes for an ultimate convergence of views. But even though authorship invariance is far from being realized in connection with the assessment of the significance of astrophysical data, no one in his right mind would conclude that astrophysics is, *ipso facto*, a subjective enterprise.

522.   A question of the form 'Is this valuation subjective or objective?" generally serves only to express a pervasive, but shallow, conceptual confusion.

523.   When I do my income tax computations, adding up long columns of figures, I add them up three times in different ways. If I get the same answer each time, that is the figure I submit. I should add that it does not help to use a computer: the problem of the correctness of the keyed in data remains. Is my evaluation of the data subjective or objective?

524.   Experiments have shown that children of the poor tend to overestimate the size of a half dollar, a largish American coin. If one who knows this, one who has not enjoyed an over opulent background, attempts to compensate for such a factor in his judgments, is he being subjective or objective in his approach?

525.   Being a tennis player, when I watch tennis matches with non tennis players, I am sometimes amused by their inability to see whether a serve is in or out. I think it would generally be ludicrous to

characterize their judgments in terms of objectivity or subjectivity. Of course, on occasion, someone may call a serve out because he passionately wants it to be out, but that is hardly the norm. The judgmental expertise of any competent tennis player really does stagger the mind: one knows almost immediately on hitting a ball whether the ball will be on or inside a line 78 feet away from one's own baseline. Are line calls in tennis a subjective matter? Sometimes a subjective aspect is prominent, sometimes not. Why should moral or scientific or philosophic valuations be any different?

526.   Rather than speaking of the subjective and the objective, it would be more sensible to recognize subjective-objective as a single coordinate in a logical space of valuations and judgments.

527.   Ethicists, some, not all, all too often wander about and thrive in a never-never land of their own contrivance, a nice place to visit, but, for the rational, not a place to reside.

528.   The same is true of those who think unrealistically of aesthetic valuations and judgments: such valuations and judgments do not differ in significant ways from ethical valuations and judgments; the symbolism and imagery is different, but the logic is not. If one wishes to explore a subjective-objective coordinate in a logical space of valuations and judgments, there is no better place to visit than the realm of art.

529.   Pointing to the middle figure in this sketch, (1),

I say to someone: "Of these three working sketches, this one, (1), is the most interesting". He looks merely puzzled and says nothing. Someone doesn't see anything to it and I see that he doesn't see. He may feel that I should say something to him. But what is there to say?

530.   To say "(1) is the most interesting" is to make an impersonal, hence somewhat abstract, judgment about (1). It is not simply to say "(1) interests me the most".

531.   There is no easy connection between what does or not interest a given individual, p, and what is or is not interesting: owing, perhaps, to personal factors, p may not be interested in a current exhibition of abstract art even though the exhibition is interesting: p is a devotee of Wyeth and Co. Conversely, p, may be interested in an exhibition even though the exhibition is deadly dull: a friend's works are being shown.

532.   If the judgment is sound, if (1) is rightly judged to be the most interesting of the three, then certain inferences are warranted.

533.   Let 'p_i' be a variable for persons, 'a_i' for acts or actions, 'c_i' for conditions and 'e_i' for entities or events; given appropriate values for p_i, a_i, c_i and e_i, e_i is rightly judged to be interesting if and only if e_i interests p_i if p_i performs a_i under c_i in connection with e_i.[56] Consequently, if e_1 is (1) and (1) is rightly judged to be the most interesting, and someone, p_1, does not find (1) to be the most interesting, then there is a problem either with p_1 or a_1 or c_1.

534.   As a painter, I would not be inclined to say anything in response to a query about my judgment that, of the three, (1) is the most interesting sketch. It is generally more sensible to do rather than to say something: there is always much that can be done and, if it were done then, after it were done, someone might say "Yes, I see" and, puzzlement past, he might come to agree that (1) is the most interesting sketch, possibly something could be made from it.

535.   Words are likely to be of no avail if the problem is that the person, p_i, is visually, or otherwise, uninformed, or if the acts or actions, a_i, that p_i performs in connection with e_i, are inappropriate, or if the conditions, c_i, under which p_i performs a_i, are somehow aberrant or infelicitous.

536.   What could be done is obvious enough: one could show him earlier and later works; one could show him predecessors and associates. One could attempt to teach him the rudiments of painting, to explore the possibilities of black pigment, black inks. Possibly one could help him learn how to look at black lines and edges and shapes. And having done all that, (years later) he might no longer have any question to ask. The question he would no longer be inclined to ask would not have been answered, but at least the inclination to ask it might have been removed.

---

[56] See Paul Ziff, *Philosophic Turnings* (Ithaca, New York: Cornell University Press, 1966) Chap. III for a discussion of related points.

537.   Still, if need be, as a painter, I could say something. So I might say: "Why is (1) the most interesting sketch? The sketch at the extreme right is over decorative, static; the one at the left is a bit all-overish, too clumsy, not quite alive, but then none of them are. Possibly something could be done with (1): It could be quickened. But to see this, one must be able to imagine the work for which (1) is only a tiny unbounded sketch, a mere notation: so imagine a 6' x 3.5' warm off-white gesso panel with the figure executed in flowing reflective glossy lamp black pigment: envisage the realization of the sketch. To do so is, no doubt, here difficult: a sketch on such a small scale is inevitably coerced when caught in the grid of a rudimentary computer graphics program. Yes, possibly (1) has some sort of life in it".

538.   An analytic philosopher is not likely to be satisfied with this sort of a response. The statement "(1) possibly has some sort of life in it, the others not" is not to be taken literally: the image, (1), engages in neither anabolic nor catabolic processes; it has no metabolism. So the image is not literally alive. And if I insist that, in contrast with the other two, (1) betrays a possibility of life, my insistence is likely to be futile. Life? Does it have vitality? That is just more of the same: nothing is to be taken literally. All talk of life here is merely metaphorical.

539.   Would it help if the metaphor were a dead metaphor? That a table has legs now gives no one pause, yet some Victorian ladies once felt obliged to skirt them, in the name of propriety. But I am not suggesting that we at once bury the problem, though in time it should be interred.

540.   What is important here is not how we categorize a statement but whether we understand it and, if we do, how we understand it and what it is we understand in understanding it. I say "This one, (1), possibly has some life in it, the others not": in so doing, I am not only endorsing my judgment that, of the three, (1) is the most interesting, I am simultaneously both judging that (1) creates a certain impression and reporting the impression that it creates.

541.   How one chooses to report an impression is largely a matter of personal style. So someone might say "Looking at (1) makes one feel

as though one were looking at something that might be or become alive"; another might say "It might be an animal of some sort", or "It seems somewhat agitated" or, depending on the impression, "It's sort of messed up in the lower half", or even "What a waste of ink and paper!" and so on. I say "(1) possibly has some life in it".

542.   Does (1) create that impression? I say so. Why does it create that impression? I don't know. Then why does it give me that impression? I don't know that either. These are matters that a philosopher should be prepared to be blank about, concerns of no concern to a painter. These questions do not pose either an artistic or a philosophic problem. (The only philosophic problem that there might be here would be a metatheoretic one: that of showing that there is no philosophic problem here.)

543.   If there is a problem here, the problem is not a problem of conceptual analysis: a detailed analytic study of what it is to be alive is not likely to make anything any clearer. If analysis of some sort is called for, what is wanted is an analysis, not of what it is to be alive, but of what it is for (1) to betray a possibility of life. That is not a philosophic problem.

544.   The requisite analysis is that that may someday be supplied by an analytic psychology of perception. Perhaps someday some psychologist will be able to say something insightful and informative about this sort of case. As a painter, I am aware of, I can attend to and I can respond to the impression; in so far as I am articulate, I can report it; as a philosopher, a spectator, I can attend to the report and hope to profit from it: in neither case do I pretend to understand the etiology of the impression. The sensitivity to impressions that painters require and frequently display is not an acquired analytic skill.

545.   A sensitivity to impressions can be cultivated. There is no mystery about that. It is cultivated by exercise: there is, as far as I know, no other way. Again, there is something to do and little to say. Here are eleven lines:

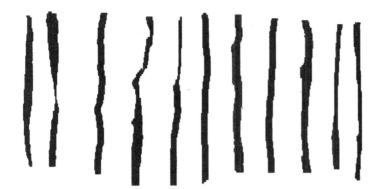

Each is different in character from the others: each has a different look. Possibly the third annoys me, the seventh and ninth I find tiresome so close together. The sixth I may find dull. Say I am blank about the others and negative about the whole: So I vary one and then another line until I arrive at this:

546.   Initially, in the process, one may feel overwhelmed by what may appear to be a superfluity of nonchoices: choices between lines that are evidently different yet whose differences seem to make no difference. But only initially: in time, perhaps after a considerable time, individual characters may begin to stand out, cooperate and constitute a whole. As one proceeds, one learns to see and, more importantly, one learns to look.

547.   It is not significant that I have been concerned with a set of lines: just so, one might juxtapose and consider a set of sentences or a set of notes; the problem merely shifts from looking to listening. In a penciled draft of her poem that begins:

"Until the Desert knows
That Water grows
His sands suffice
But let him once suspect
That Caspian Fact
Sahara dies"

Emily Dickinson had written down four alternative versions for the sixth line: "Contentment dies", "Creation dies", "His status dies", "Standard denies".[57]

548.   "Did she make the right choice?" How is that to be established? These are not questions that, here and now, actually confront us; they are, at best and as yet, only idle: for what provokes them? The mere existence of alternatives is not enough. Anyway, it is never possible to prove that a judgment is sound: all that one can ever aspire to is this: to find nothing that suffices to fault it.[58]

549.   Sometimes the source of an impression lends itself to analysis, sometimes not. Two types of cases are worth citing here: that of the chicken sexer and that of the cow man.

550.   The chicken sexer: in the poultry industry it is important to determine the sex of new born chicks. This can be done by a direct anatomical examination; such an examination, however, takes time and requires manipulating the chicks. To reduce the time and eliminate the manipulation, persons, and in particular, Japanese, are trained to determine the sex of a chick simply on the basis of a visual inspection. This is done by showing them boxes of male chicks and

---

[57] See Thomas H. Johnson (ed.), *The Poems of Emily Dickinson* (Cambridge, Mass.: Harvard University Press, 1963) Vol. III, 896.

[58] See Paul Ziff, *Epistemic Analysis* (Dordrecht, Holland: D. Reidel Pub. Co., 1984) 137 ff.

boxes of female chicks. After a time the chicken sexers can tell, fairly well (possibly with about eighty percent accuracy), simply by the look of a chick whether it is male or female. However, when they are asked what it is about the look that indicates the sex of the chick, they are incapable of saying. Apparently chicks may have a male look or a female look, but what makes a look one or the other is not known. Just so, I can often tell just by the look of a drawing that it is a Klee drawing, but what makes that look the look of a Klee is not something that I can say. There are indefinitely many looks that do not, at present, lend themselves to any sort of analysis. Perhaps they never will.[59]

551.   The case of the cow man is contrariwise: many years ago, when I was at the University of Wisconsin, there was a foreign bovine expert visiting the agricultural school. He was able to tell, simply on the basis of a visual inspection, whether a cow had recently calved, what its milk production had been, what it was likely to be and so forth. But, unlike the chicken sexers, he was able to indicate, and in great detail, precisely which visual aspects of the cow provided the basis of his conclusions. Just so, one can sometimes say why a certain painting creates the impression it does.[60]

552.   What is the difference between (1) and the other two? The difference is, evidently, differences in lines, edges and shapes. But since there are many, more than are needed here, let us focus down to but one: the difference between the upper and lower half of the sketch is less subtle, more pronounced, in (1) than in the other two. Here one could say: I am not simply reporting an impression but, also, providing a description, making an objective statement.

553.   When I offer such a description, one may be inclined to say: "In that, there may be a fact of the matter." But when I report an impression, when I say "This one, (1), possibly has some life in it, the others not", some are inclined to say: "In that, there is no fact of the matter." So one can be tempted to suppose that there is some

---

[59] See Paul Ziff, *Antiaesthetics* (Dordrecht, Holland: D. Reidel Pub. Co., 1984) 69 ff.

[60] See *Op. cit.*, 80.

wonderfully sharp and significant line to be discerned dividing reports of impressions from descriptions.

554.   To say "the difference is more pronounced" is not simply to offer a description: it is also to report an impression. However, in this case, at least, that which gives rise to the impression may seem clear enough: there is more black ink in the lower than in the upper half of the sketch in the middle.

555.   But how is that determined? Perhaps by squaring off the figures and drawing a bisecting line thus:

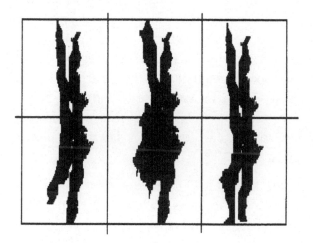

Then, given that one is working with computer graphics, one could do a count of the number of black pixels in the top halves and then compare them with the number in the bottom halves. One could, and no doubt that statement of a possibility is somehow comforting; but, in fact, one doesn't count anything: one simply uses one's eyes and reports an impression. (And, in fact, counting proves nothing: there are the same number of black pixels in the top as in the bottom half of the following diagram:

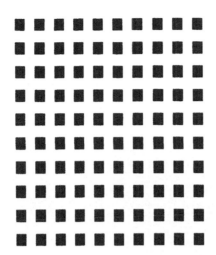

yet I should be reluctant to say that the top is as pronounced as the bottom.)

556.   One impression may cohere with another. If one compares figure (1), the one in the middle, with an upside down version of it, the greater weight of the bottom half is at once apparent:

The reason is, of course, that the bottom half of a painting can bear more weight than the top; in consequence, the apparent weight of a shape is increased when the shape is shifted from bottom to top. But what is apparent weight? Shapes in a sketch do not literally have weight; so, again, one is, at best, only reporting an impression.

557.   Is the judgment that (1) possibly has some life in it somehow at fault? How is one to say? Perhaps it would help to compare the following two, (2) and (3):

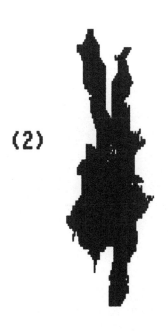

(2)

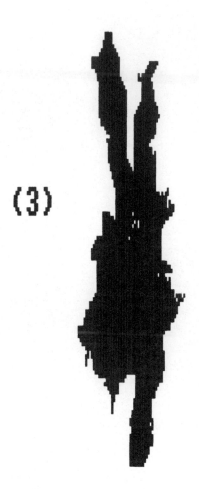

(3)

The fundamental difference between (2) and (3) is simply the factor of size: here I take it that, if one must choose between the two, the larger one, (3), is the one more plausibly characterized in terms of "alive". One might think that, as a philosopher, the question "Which is more alive?" should strike me as somewhat absurd and, anyway, unanswerable; but it does not: the question awaits an impression and solicits both a judgment and a report of that impression; as a painter, one susceptible to such impressions, I have no difficulty in making

such a judgment and providing such a report: (3) is more alive than
(2). The shapes are organic, suggestive of a large animal; so the more
the image is "as large as life", the more alive it may appear. Perhaps.
Again, one may be inclined to ask: "How is such a judgment to be
supported?" But, again, the locus of an answer lies in a question: what
suggests that the judgment is at fault?

558.   I say to someone: Look at this jaunty creature! (4):

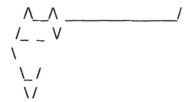

559.   "What jaunty creature?" he replies. I say: Look at this other
creature! (5):

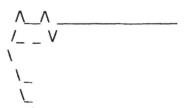

560.   I judge that (4) is jauntier, more cheerful than (5). Does
someone disagree? Suppose someone does. Someone replies "What
creatures?" He contends that (4) and (5) are no more than lines and
shapes: all talk of "creatures" is simply otiose. Furthermore, if,
willfully, one takes either set of lines and shapes to be a creature, then
either can be characterized as being the jauntier, the more cheerful. My
judgment is, he contends, merely arbitrary.

561.   Is the judgment that (5) is a creature at fault? There is, as far as
I can see, no reasonably effective procedure for establishing that (5)
either is or is not any sort of creature. Of course (5) is constituted of
lines and shapes: so people are constituted of flesh and skin and bones.
Skin and bones do not think, yet people do; lines and shapes are not a
creature, yet (5) is: one can point here and there and say: this is an ear,

this another, this an eye, that the nose, though there is a possibility that the nose is not a nose but a mouth, and so on.

562.   When I look at (5), I do not see the lines and shapes in (5) as a creature: on the contrary, I simply see a creature. When I look at the single shape below the eyes, I mostly see it as a nose, but, on occasion, I see it as a mouth. 'Seeing as' seems singularly inappropriate in the absence of attractive alternatives.

563.   What does one see in figure (6)?

(6)

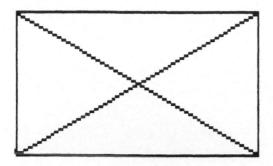

If I were looking at a geometry text, I might see only a simple quadrilateral with two inscribed diagonals. But in the context of this essay, I see it as various triangles, or as a solid object, a pyramid seen from above, or as an envelope or as a view of a hallway receding in the distance.

564.   It has been said that:

> "There is not in all the world's criticism a single purely descriptive statement concerning which one is prepared to say beforehand, "If it is true, I shall like that work so much the better"... ."[61]

---

[61] A. Isenberg, "Critical Communication," *The Philosophical Review*, vol. 58 (1949).

565.   If that were true then, I suppose, one who gives it credence should be inclined to say that the statement "(5) is a creature and (4) is a jauntier one" is not "a purely descriptive statement": it seems plausible to suppose that someone should like (4) and (5) "so much the better" if (4) and (5) were creatures rather than not creatures but only collections of lines and shapes.

566.   Is (5) a creature and (4) a jauntier one? There is no way to prove it. After all, I am inclined to judge that (5) is a creature and (4) a jauntier one owing to the way they look to me, thus owing simply to impressions. No doubt others may be subject to similar impressions, but what would that signify? Should one count noses here? Could the soundness, the objectivity, of a judgment consist in nothing more than a number of noses all snorting in agreement? Again, one must, of course, go another way: if nothing genuinely calls the judgment into question then what is there to be concerned with? Someone's remarkable incapacity to comprehend such a sketch would hardly persuade one that the sketch is incomprehensible.

567.   I say to someone: Look at these two triangles!

(7)

    O   O

O O   O   O

one is possibly isosceles, the other not.

568.   But there are, someone might reply, merely six capital 'O"s in the figure. Are there triangles there? And anyway, triangles are, after all, abstract mathematical entities, altogether nonvisible. What color is a triangle?

569.   Perhaps the statement that there are at least two triangles in (7) is not "a purely descriptive statement". If so, one need not ignore the fact that it is evidently not a fact that being "purely descriptive" is an important attribute of a statement: such a categorization yields no significant partitioning of true and untrue statements.

570.   That there are (at least) two triangles in (7), to be seen in (7), is, in one way or another, and in some sense or other, undoubtedly

true, but the statement that there are cannot readily be construed as "a
purely descriptive statement". (Or at least I think it cannot: I would not
claim to have any clear understanding of the significance of the phrase
'purely descriptive statement'. I invoke this bit of jargon only to revoke
any license for its use in this context.)

571.   (This, however, is not to grant that all abstract entities are
nonvisible. So long as there is, say, a wooden table before you, it has a
surface, and though one may sand off the surface of the table, a surface
remains so long as the table remains and that surface, the surface that
inevitably remains so long as the table remains, is an abstract entity yet
eminently visible. Or, to invoke another obvious example, consider a
sharp edge of a shape in a lithograph: that edge is an interface between
the shape and that which is not the shape, a two dimensional entity,
abstract yet visible.)

572.   There is a simple reasonable procedure for confirming the
statement that, of the two triangles in (7), at least one is possibly
isosceles. So one proceeds by drawing lines (a) and (b) as in (8):

(8)

                    O   O
             (a) / \ (b)
              /O O\   O   O

and then determining that (a) and (b) are equal in length. Yet the
procedure displayed in (8) is certainly open to question: it is question
begging in that it presupposes that there are, in fact, two triangles in
(7).

573.   There are, one might say, simply six 'O''s in (7), nothing more.
Of course, each 'O' could be taken to be an oversized point and, if so,
and if one is so inclined, one could then project many triangles, at least
two of which would be isosceles.

574.   Whether there are only two or rather more triangles in a figure like (7), a figure constituted of six 'O''s, could be made more or less plausible by simple variations in the arrangement of the 'O''s. Thus (9):

(9)   O   O

              O O   O O

is plausibly immediately characterizable as two, but not more than two, triangles.

575.   Yet not only is there no reasonably effective procedure for determining whether or not (7) is constituted of two, or more than two, triangles, there is no procedure at all for such a determination. Thus (10), construed as a variant of (7),

(10)   O O

              O O O O

has evidently lost the immediate character of a pair of triangles and has acquired that of a trapezoid, and this for a reason that is altogether explicable, yet not a reason that is associated with a procedure. The report "The six 'O''s are too close together" is not a procedural result. Or if it is, then there is a procedure for determining that image (1) is possibly alive: just look and see!

576.   I say to someone: Look at this straight line (11):

(11)   _____

and he replies: "Yes, that is a straight line." So we agree that (11) is a straight line, but perhaps we do not agree about (5) being a creature or about (4) being a jauntier one or possibly about the triangles in (7), and certainly we may not agree about the possibility of life in (1).

577.   I say that (1) has the possibility of life, that (5) is a creature, that (4) is a jauntier one, that there are two triangles in (7), one of which is possibly isosceles, and that (11) is a straight line. Thus I make various and distinct judgments. That the judgment about (11) is unobjectionable, and presumably at the objective end of the

subjective-objective coordinate, seems to be reasonably clear. Why is it not equally clear that the judgments about (4), (5) and (7) are unobjectionable? And is the judgment about the possibility of life in (1) hopelessly at risk?[62]

578.   What is significant here is not whether or not the statement that (11) is a straight line is "a purely descriptive statement" but, perhaps rather, whether there is an effective procedure for confirming it. And there is, or anyway, there seems to be.

579.   One lays a standard straight edge, a ruler, alongside the line and then sees, judges, whether the points on the line are equidistant from the points along the edge of the straight edge.

580.   Such a procedure might, however, be better characterized, not simply as an effective, but, rather, as a reasonably effective procedure, for one need not ignore the fact that one must simply see whether the points on the line are equidistant from the points along the edge of the straight edge: for that there is no procedure. (In any effective procedure there is always a step for which there is no effective procedure, but whether the procedure is an effective procedure or merely a reasonably effective procedure depends on how and when one is forced to make that step.) (In aesthetics, as in ethics, it is essential to adopt and display a democratic attitude, to render irreverence to rulers.)

581.   One must simply see: but what does one see? Look at (12):

(12)   ••

(11) is a straight line, but so is (12). There seems to be no objection to the judgment that (11) is a straight line, but what about (12)? Does it depend on how closely one looks? When looked at up close, very very

---

62 See *Epistemic Analysis*, 176 ff.

close, (11) is a variant of (12), while (12) looked at up close, very close, is (13):

(13)

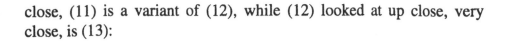

582. Seated high up in a football stadium, one might say "The players are the size of ants." One knows that of course they are not: the players merely look to be the size that ants look to be when one sees ants as one ordinarily sees them. But (12) is a straight line although (12) is, one might say, in fact, in some sense, (13), yet (13) is not a straight line but, rather, a series of rectangles lined up in a row. Is the judgment that (12) is a straight line at fault?

583. Consider figure (14):

(14)

There are at least seven elements (lines or rectangles?) in (14), but are there also eight? Staring at a railway track disappearing in the distance, someone might say: "There, at the horizon, the train must become a monorail."

584. An excessive respect for procedures is of a piece with being overawed by proofs.

585. The proof, (15):   (a) *P* is true.

(b) If *P* is true then *Q* is true.

Therefore (z): *Q* is true.

is pristine and impeccable, an exemplification of the use of modus ponens: "The judgment that (15) is valid" one might say "is not to be questioned." But is it beyond question? How is that to be established? Perhaps the proof is no proof but merely an instantiation of a fallacy of equivocation.

586.   The validity of (15) rests on a fundamental notational assumption, an assumption in virtue of which the expression 'P' in line (a) stands for whatever the expression 'P' in line (b) stands for: that fundamental assumption is neither stated nor, without incurable circularity, statable. For, of course, if one adds premise (c):

(c) 'P' in (a) stands for whatever 'P' in (b) stands for.

then one is assuming that the expression "P" at the left in (c) stands for whatever the expression "P" to the right in (c) stands for; one is also assuming that the expression '(a)' in (c) stands for whatever the expression '(a)' in (15) stands for. (Thus a common misconception of Tarski's brilliant *Wahrheitsbegriff* arises from a failure to realize that the statement "Snow is white' is true if and only if snow is white' cannot sensibly be represented as of the form "P' is true if and only if P', which would be to say, absurdly, that the letter 'P' is true if and only if P. A more felicitous representation of it, and one which at once poses the problems of generalization, would be 'S is true if and only if P'.)

587.   The principle of identity, a=a, is a fundamental law of logic, but the formal statement of that law of logic, owing to the limitations inherent in any symbolic system, is inherently circular. It is an assumption of standard notation that the expression 'a' appearing on one part of a page be the same as the expression 'a' appearing on another part of the page.[63] (It is perhaps worth noting that there are formal notations in which such an assumption is not satisfied in certain trivial cases. Thus, for example, in APL, a powerful computer programming language, it is possible to determine that a=1 and that

---

[63] The *locus classicus* of this point is Alonzo Church's "Set of Postulates", *The Annals of Mathematics*, 1932.

b=1, yet a<>b. The reason for this is simply that in APL no visual difference is made between '1' as a scalar and '1' as a vector. But this trifling instance of homonymy poses no problems for an experienced user of the language.)

588.   Is there in reading a logic text an effective procedure for determining when such an assumption is and when it is not warranted?

Is that a statement of the law of identity? And is this?

And this?

a =   a

Certainly this is not:

a =

                       a

Perhaps there is no fact of the matter about the soundness of such judgments. Logic texts are, after all, sublime artifacts of an abstract art: the art of reasoning.

589.   The main thesis of this essay is that, although there are many different and conflicting moralities, some of them can be shown to be mistaken, on rational grounds. So far, in the course of this essay, I have not provided a single example of a morality that can be shown to be mistaken on rational grounds.

590.   To establish that a given morality is mistaken on rational grounds, one could attempt to establish that the morality is either logically incoherent, or inconsistent or radically incomplete. It is easy enough to contrive artificial, although conceivably real, examples.

591.   Suppose someone holds that it is absolutely wrong to kill anything: he holds to the principle that it is wrong to kill and this principle is not subject to defeasibility conditions. He also holds that it is not wrong to kill game. Obviously, he has an inconsistent and irrational morality.

592.   Such artificial, although conceivably real, examples are, however, of no genuine interest here. They merely point to logical possibilities. What is wanted is an undoubtedly real and pertinent example of a morality that can be held to be mistaken on rational grounds.

593.   To find such an example, one must consider not simply the enjoinders and evaluations that serve to constitute the morality in question, but also the overall conceptual scheme of the persons having the morality in question. As I said previously, if a group complies with a moral code, the judgments, evaluations, behavior, attitudes, inclinations and so forth of the group accordingly exemplify a distinct and specific structuring constitutive of compliance with the code. But a person's behavior, attitudes, inclinations and so forth are structured, not only by the person's moral code, but also by the person's overall conceptual scheme.

594.   For example, the Jains of India held that it was wrong to kill anything: nonetheless, they practiced self-mortification and they also,

of course, ate. Of course, they did not know that in practicing self-mortification they were killing bacteria, cells etc. on their bodies; nor did they know that in eating they were probably killing living cells.

595.   If, today, a knowledgeable and scientifically well-informed person were to attempt to adhere to the morality of the Jains, one would have to say that the person was irrational and has a morality that can be held to be mistaken on rational grounds. For such a person to attempt to adhere to the morality of the Jains would be a logical absurdity: if, knowing that in eating he was killing living cells, he refused to eat, he would then, knowingly, be killing himself. Hence he would have to deem it wrong to eat and wrong not to eat.

596.   Before trying to present a genuinely interesting example of a mistaken morality, I want to consider a morality that most people today in America reject, even though the morality cannot be shown to be mistaken on rational grounds.

597.

> "To the mind of the simple, unsophisticated Shaker it seems marvelously inconsistent for any human government to be administered for the sole benefit of its own officers and their particular friends and favorites; or that more than one half the citizens should be disfranchised because they happen to be females, and compelled by the sword to obey laws they never sanctioned, and ofttimes in which they have no faith, and to submit to taxation where there has been no previous representation; while still millions of other fellow-citizens are treated as property, because they chance to possess a darker-colored skin than their cruel brethren. And again, that the members (brethren and sisters) of the same religious body or church should be divided into rich and poor in the things of this temporary world, but who are vainly expecting that, in the

world to come, they shall be willing to have eternal things in common!"[64]

598.   The Shakers were religious communists: they were committed to the sharing of all property. They were committed to the equality of women and men. They were committed to the equality of races. They were opposed to the abuse of animals: in time, they became vegetarians. They were also opposed to generation: they practiced, and were committed to, celibacy.

599.

> "The Shakers testify that they, as a people, find more pleasure and enjoyment -real good - arising from the celibate spiritual union of the sexes, and more of an absence of the afflictions and annoyances -real evil - arising from the generative union of the sexes, than, as they believe, is ever experienced in the order of the world."[65]

600.   The Shaker way of life seems to me to be altogether admirable in most respects, though not all. However, I admire it from afar: I am not, and would not be, a Shaker.

601.   Why not? In part, because of Shakerism's religiosity: "... all Shaker communities are essentially religious institutions."[66] Members of the Society were required to "... conform to the moral and religious principles of the institution."[67] Since I am an utterly irreligious person, I am clearly not qualified to be a Shaker. (Let me note that one of Mother Lee's fundamental religious beliefs would not trouble me. Ann Lee was the founder, and spiritual mother, of Shakerism. She believed that Jesus was alive within her. Despite my irreligiosity, I have no quarrel with that particular belief. There is a very simple accommodating transformation that serves to resolve this apparent

---

[64] F. W. Evans, Shakers *Compendium*, (New Lebanon, N. Y., 1867) 54-55.

[65] *Op. cit.*, 39.

[66] F. W. Evans, Shakers *Compendium*, (New Lebanon, N. Y., 1867) 43.

[67] *Op. cit.*, 40.

conceptual conflict: for 'Jesus' read 'an appreciation of life' and all is easy.)

602.   I would not, indeed, could not, be a Shaker for two other very simple reasons. I could not commit myself either to a communal life style or to celibacy: the latter strikes me as unwarranted, the former as impossible for me.

603.   I simply could not live a communal life style. I have no objection to an equitable distribution of goods, but I require my own house and my own private space, a place in which I can think and work. In my set of values, these have a very high priority ranking. I am not a social being. Neither do I have "the gift of being simple" (a deservedly famous Shaker song): I prefer the complex and the abstruse. I would not wish to dine in the communal hall. (If Hilbert, Minkowski, Szilard and John Austin were fellow diners, the matter might be otherwise. If Fermat were there and would give me his proof of his last theorem, I would certainly attend.)

604.   I find it almost impossible even to imagine what the world would be like if there were an equitable distribution of goods in accordance with the principles of Shakerism. Certainly many people would be much better off than they are now, but, just as certainly, many people would be, or would deem themselves to be, much worse off than they are now.

605.   Are there any rational grounds to object to the Shaker's communal principles and practices?

606.   Shakerism has not survived: there are now no Shaker communes in America. One may be inclined to say that, given the greed that is endemic in this world, there was no possibility of Shakerism surviving. Possibly greed was a major factor contributing to the demise of Shakerism. But one can hardly criticize a morality on the ground that it is opposed to, and comes into conflict with, greed. Or can one?

607.   Let S be an ideal Shaker, a member of a commune and one whose values are dictated by the Shaker morality. Consider the set $\{Vs\}$, the set of S's values ordered in terms of S's presumed priorities.

It seems reasonable to suppose that the continued existence of Shaker communes would be of intrinsic value to S and that it would have a very high priority ranking. Let ve be that value; hence ve is a member of $\{Vs\}$. Given that, as a Shaker, S is committed to the sharing of all property, to an equitable distribution of goods, communal ownership of property must also be one S's intrinsic values, and it, too, must have a very high priority ranking. Let vp be that value; hence vp is also a member of $\{Vs\}$. Finally, let vc be the intrinsic value of celibacy: vc must also be a member of $\{Vs\}$. The set of values, $\{Vs\}$, may then seem to be open to criticism on the ground of the incompatibility of its members. Isn't there something of an incompatibility between the achievement of ve, the achievement of vp and the achievement of vc? Since the Shakers do not procreate, the only way for the communes to acquire new members, thus to continue to exist, is by having outsiders voluntarily join the communes. To give up one's property and become celibate, however, is not an attractive act to the persons of this world dedicated to the acquisition of money and goods.

608.   I am inclined to think, however, that the preceding argument is spurious. In time people change, and during the time that Shakerism flourished, one of the communes had over one thousand members. Had there then been a genuine incompatibility between ve, vp and vc, no such commune could have existed. Today, of course, Shakerism is impossible in America: we live under an oligarchy of the world's corporations and communism is the nightmare of all corporate dreamers. The Shaker's cross has been replaced by the dollar sign.

609.   If there are rational grounds to object to Shaker communism, I do not know what they are.

610.   As for celibacy, I think it would be most marvelous if most of the world's population, particularly the impoverished inhabitants of this world, those incapable of caring for their offspring, were to practice celibacy, at least for a few generations. There would then be an enormous reduction in the world's population and a consequent reduction in human misery: children of the impoverished are all too likely to lead short and utterly miserable lives.

611. Possibly I could practice celibacy, but I see no reason, none at all, why I should commit myself to resisting a fundamental biological urge.

612. I could not be a Shaker and, of course, no Shaker commune would have accepted me as a member, and rightfully so. That, however, is simply a fact about me. The significant question still is: are there any rational grounds for rejecting the morality of the Shakers?

613. First, consider the two principles, (C) and (R):

(C) One should not copulate.

(R) One should not reproduce.

The Shakers were clearly committed to principle (C); but were they also committed to the non-reproduction of the species? Possibly they never thought about artificial insemination, and certainly they never thought about cloning. It seems reasonable to suppose, however, given the historical position of the Shakers, that a commitment to (C) did, in fact, entail a commitment to (R).

614. Secondly, the Shakers certainly held that it was morally right to be a Shaker, at least that it was not morally wrong. Furthermore, it was morally right for anyone, and for everyone, to be a Shaker, at least it was not morally wrong.

615. This means, however, that the Shaker morality gives moral sanction to the voluntary, and, from an evolutionary point of view, virtually immediate, demise of the species.

616. Of course, the Shakers gave some thought to this matter:

"The trite old question is sometimes raised, "What would become of the world if all were to become Shakers?" In view of the condition of a good part of the people in it, the thought has sometimes suggested itself that it might not be a bad idea to let the world run out. But there is not the least danger of the world's population failing from religious motives, nor is there any fear that all mankind will become Shakers in this life."[68]

617.   Whether it is a good or a bad idea to let the world run out is really of no consequence: it will run out, be burnt up, when our Sun turns into a white giant and then a red dwarf. Meanwhile we have lives to lead. That there is no fear that "all mankind will become Shakers" is altogether irrelevant. The fact of the matter is that the Shaker morality does sanction the voluntary demise, the virtually immediate demise, of all mankind.

618.   Are there any rational grounds to object to that? It is certainly not irrational for any given individual to decide not to procreate, not to participate in the reproduction of the species. If everyone else arrived at the same decision, would the decision not to procreate then become irrational? I see no reason to think so.

619.   From a social point of view, one could say that the society was, in effect, committing suicide; but whatever objections there may be to the suicide of individuals, I do not see how they could be relevant in this case. This "societal suicide" would place no burdens on survivors; neither would it constitute the shirking of responsibilities. Nor could one, in such a case, speak of obligations to the unborn, to future generations: if there is to be no procreation, then there are no unborn, no future generations to consider.

620.   I cannot criticize this aspect of the morality of the Shakers on any rational basis. I can criticize it on the basis of my own personal morality. I am committed to an appreciation of life, of all life, and thus to an appreciation of human life. Any morality that sanctions the end of all human life is, *ipso facto*, in full conflict with my morality.

621.   Shakerism constitutes an alternative morality that I cannot criticize or condemn on any rational basis. In consequence, I have no

---

[68] Anna White and Leila S. Taylor, *Shakerism* (Press of Fred J. Her, Columbus, Ohio, 1904) 281.

warrant, other than my own morality, for saying that the morality of Shakerism is mistaken, or that it is in error or that it is wrong.

622.   Of course I cannot prove that there are no rational grounds on the basis of which one can criticize the morality of the Shakers. I can only say that I know of no such grounds, despite having looked long and hard for them. I do not believe that they exist.

623.   To find a genuinely interesting example of a mistaken morality, we must think about killing.

624.   Is it wrong to kill anything without good and sufficient reason?

625.   Since most people evidently do not think it is wrong to kill mosquitoes, flies, ants and other insects, and a great many do not think it is wrong to kill various fowls and mammals, my question would no doubt be more poignant for many if it were: is it wrong to kill a person without good and sufficient reason? (I, personally, am indifferent to the difference.)

626.   Suppose I am on a fast moving train; an exit door is, owing to some mechanical defect, standing open, a person is at the door. He and I are alone in the car. I do not know him and I know nothing about him. For no reason at all, I push him out of the door and he is killed. Is what I did wrong?

627.   What a person judges to be right or wrong depends on his or her morality. If someone says that what I did is wrong but does not know why such an act is wrong, then that person has no clear conception of what is right or of what is wrong: the person has no clear understanding of his or her own morality.

628.   Here one cannot consider the consequences, or even the expected consequences, of the act for, by hypothesis, the consequences are unknown and the act was simply impulsive and utterly mindless. (Conceivably, the consequences of the act could be beneficial to the society: the person killed was an assassin on his way to perform some socially malevolent deed. Conceivably, the consequences of the act could be to the detriment of the killer. The person killed was on his

way to make a will endowing all his considerable monies and goods to the killer, who happened to be a long lost relative.)

629.   Here, perhaps, some would be inclined to say "It just is wrong to kill a person without any reason at all!" Even if that is true, it does not constitute an answer to the question: Why is it wrong?

630.   "There must be some warrant for killing a person!" The question remains: Why?

631.   Here I am not interested in "religious" or "authoritarian" answers to the question: "God forbids it!", "My Guru forbids it!". There are no supernatural beings, and that an authority says that something is wrong does not show that it is morally wrong. Nor does the fact that an authority authorized a killing ("Der Führer", the Grand Dragon of the KKK, the State) show that it is morally right.

632.   Here some might say "I am simply committed to the principle that it is wrong to kill a person without any reason." That one is committed to some principle does not mean that such a commitment is, *ipso facto*, a rational commitment. A devout member of some cult, perhaps a worshipper of Kali, the Hindu goddess of destruction, could conceivably be committed to the principle that it is right to kill anyone, with or without a reason. (Of course, not even the Thugees of India killed without any reason at all: assassination for profit was for them a religious duty.)

633.   "To do something without any reason at all is irrational!" That is plainly untrue. When I stroll through my garden, I often clasp my hands behind my back. I do it without thinking. I have no reason for doing that, yet I often do it. Am I being irrational? Surely not! All of us do all sorts of things all the time without any reason at all: we cross our legs, we take deep breaths, we look about, we mutter imprecations when we view television commercials, propaganda.

634.   To deny that when we do these things we have a reason to do them is not to deny that are reasons why we do them. Reasons to do something are personal and depend on the subject. If I have a reason to go to Verona, it does not follow that you have a reason to go to Verona. The reason is "my reason". In contrast, a reason why

something is so, or is done, is impersonal and does not depend on the subject. Strictly speaking, nothing is ever "my reason" why some event occurred.

635.   There is, however, a profound difference between doing these familiar things that we do without any reason at all and killing something, a person, an ant, without any reason at all. Those things that I, and many others, do without any reason at all are not for me, or for many others, either morally or socially significant acts or actions. In contrast, the killing of anything is, for me, always a morally significant act, and, for many persons, the killing of a person is likely to be both a morally and socially significant act. (Unfortunately, not for all: there are monsters in our midst; one need only think of the atrocities so casually committed in Germany, Cambodia, Rwanda.)

636.   If an act is a significant act, it must signify something. It has been said that "life is a tale told by an idiot, full of sound and fury, signifying nothing", but, even if that were true, taking any life would, nonetheless, be a significant act signifying that that life was without any value.

637.   To kill a person is to perform a significant act. It is not like strolling through one's garden with hands clasped behind one's back. To perform an act of such significance without any reason, knowing nothing at all about the person, is, I think, plainly irrational. The critical factor here is that the act is significant: the malevolence or benevolence of the act is irrelevant. For example, *The Massachusetts Society for the Prevention of Cruelty to Animals* is an altogether admirable society. Nonetheless, to donate a billion dollars to that society without any reason to do so, without giving any thought to what one is doing, would be irrational. (To prove this, I suppose one would have to undertake an analysis of the common conception of rationality. I am not concerned to do so: such a "proof" would be as useful, and is as necessary, as a "proof" that 2+2=4. (And let me say that, if I could, I would donate huge sums to the *MSPCA*: constrained by economic factors, my contributions have not been impressive. But, as Yogi Berra might have said, I can only do what I can do.))

638.   However, not all irrational acts are immoral. Suppose a person, on his way to a racetrack, sees a license plate with the letters "FIX" and also discovers that a horse named "FIX" is running; he at once decides to bet a huge sum on the horse without bothering to learn anything about the horse or the odds: I would say that that person is behaving irrationally. I would not say that he is behaving immorally. (Some hold gambling to be immoral: many do not.) Betting on a horse race is not, in and of itself, a morally or socially significant act. Killing a person is.

639.   To kill a person without any reason is an utterly irrational act.

640.   To kill anything, say a mosquito, without any reason is irrational. It implicates the judgment that the life that is taken is essentially and necessarily without any value: given that the act is performed without any reason, there can be no rational basis for such a judgment. (Some years ago an experiment was performed in the Everglades. A powerful loud speaker was set up which broadcasted a mating cry of a mosquito. An electrified screen was placed in front of the speaker. Thousands of mosquitoes responded to the cry and were electrocuted. Fortunately, that experiment did not provide a means of killing all the mosquitoes in the Everglades, the reason being that there are something like twenty thousand different mating cries that mosquitoes respond to. I say fortunately, for the destruction of the mosquitoes would cause a profound, and probably disastrous, alteration of the Everglades ecosystem: the food chain of the animals would be thoroughly disrupted.)

641.   A rational person must deem it irrational deliberately to kill anything without good and sufficient reason.

642.   To ask the hard question here is easy: what counts as "good and sufficient reason"?

643.   People kill other people for an indefinite variety of "reasons": because the person snored, is a Jew, is a communist, looked at my girl friend, called me a bastard, wouldn't give me his money, is black, had a squint, stirred her tea with her left hand and just about any "reason" one can think of.

644.   Not all of these would be accredited "reasons". A reason to perform an act or action is a fact about performance that induces, or tends to induce, a rational person to perform. A person on trial for killing his Aunt might say "My reason for doing her in was that she stirred her tea with her left hand." One could say of him "There was no reason for him to kill his Aunt, but his reason, the reason he gave the court, was that she stirred her tea with her left hand".

645.   That someone said to me "Your mother is a whore" would not, for me, be a reason to kill him. However, I have no doubt that for some, perhaps even many, that would constitute a sufficient reason to kill. Unfortunately, we live in a society in which the response to negative emotive language is likely to be instant aggression.

646.   Let M be one person, X another and J still another. X is a Nazi, and learning that J is of Jewish descent, deems that to be a good and sufficient reason to kill J. M, rightly, deems it to be no reason at all for killing J. Do X and M have different and conflicting moralities? I do not think so.

647.   Is the fact that J is of Jewish descent a reason for X to kill J? I see no way of denying that, for X, it is a reason. In killing J, X would be killing a person of Jewish descent: that fact about the performance of the act induces X to perform it. Is X being irrational? Monstrous certainly, but not as far as I can see, immediately irrational, which is not to deny that underlying irrational beliefs are undoubtedly implicated.

648. X has a reason to kill J, but not a good reason and certainly not a sufficient reason. Why not?

649.   Here one must consider why, for X, the fact that J is of Jewish descent constitutes a reason for X to kill J. The obvious answer, suggested by Nazi atrocities, is that anyone of Jewish descent is a threat to the society, and only by killing such persons can this threat be eliminated. Hence, killing J is justifiable on the grounds of self-defense.

650.   Self-defense, and self-preservation, broadly construed to include one's family, friends and society, and benevolent euthanasia

are, as far as my own morality, and that of many others, is concerned, the only justifiable grounds for killing anything. As far as morality is concerned, I see no difference between the morality of the Nazis and my own morality.

651.   Of course, I am not a Nazi: I believe that the beliefs of the Nazis are utterly irrational. That a person is of Jewish descent, is African and so forth in no way warrants the belief that the person is a threat to the society, and even if the person were a threat to society, that in no way would warrant killing the person. A difference in beliefs, however, does not, *ipso facto*, constitute a difference in morality.

652.   To find a genuinely alternative and irrational morality, one must look at a morality prevalent here in America.

653.   Before proceeding, however, I want to pause for a moment to take a broader look at and gain a perspective on the moralities in America. I do not think that one can think sensibly about such moral matters without casting an eye at the realities of life here and now: one must look at and attend to the position that one finds oneself in.

654.   That all persons are born unequal, and are endowed by their society with altogether alienable and unequal rights, is a portentous truth that one must confront in a study of a morality in America.

655.   The initial source of inequalities is to be found in the differences between zygotes, differences characterizable in genetic terms but attributable to innumerable factors. Thereafter, owing to interactions with profoundly different ecosystems, inequalities accrete and grow, until canceled in death.

656.   That "all men are created equal" is, at best, a political slogan, a rallying cry; it is difficult to see how anyone could ever have taken it seriously. Jeremy Bentham, sensible man that he was, on reading American proclamations, proclaimed them to be "contemptible nonsense on stilts". (Nonsense abounds in our publicly and legally accredited declarations. Consider the "Pledge of Allegiance" which school children are required to pronounce: "I pledge allegiance to the flag *and* to the republic for which it stands." It is the conjunction "and"

that produces the nonsense: how can one pledge allegiance to a symbol, to a piece of cloth? And then, in a court of law, one is required to "Swear to tell the truth, the whole truth and nothing but the truth." Only one who believed himself to be infallible could honestly swear to tell the truth: the best that I could do is to swear to tell what I believe to be the truth. And as for "the whole truth": who knows the whole truth about anything?)

657.   That persons are unequal is an obvious truth: less obvious is the fact that their inequalities include inequalities of rights, duties, obligations, freedoms, liberties and so forth. These inequalities are then perpetuated, celebrated and enshrined in moral, legal and diverse behavioral codes and practices.

658.   One born of rich parents can enjoy and exercise the much vaunted American moral and political rights to life, liberty and the pursuit of happiness: a black of the ghetto must struggle merely to survive. The former is born to a life of privilege guaranteed by legal rights of property and inheritance. The latter is born to a life of penury; having nothing, his legal rights of property and inheritance, having vacuous domain, can hardly be exercised: the rights of others are apt to be exercised against him.

659.   Here, in America, a god fearing society, statistics indicate that the likelihood of survival is greater when one is with strangers than when one is with friends or relations: sociobiologists may mutter about kin-selection, but we Americans have managed to make murder a friendly family practice. However, among strangers, the likelihood of being raped, mugged, or subjected to various other types of felonious assault is, at present, also considerable and appears to be constantly increasing.

660.   A termination of one's existence is fearful to most, desirable to some and a matter of indifference to others.

661.   Generally, people seem to know that they are going to die, that being, perhaps, the easiest of all inductions, but few seem to equate their inevitable death with the cessation of their own existence. Being subject to, and manifesting, motivated irrationality, most believe in spirits and spiritual survival. Some believe they will live another life

in a spiritual world. Some believe they will be reincarnated in this world. In these matters, few have any care for, or even any conception of, reasons or evidence. Their spiritual beliefs are not subject to rational restraints. Hardly any have any conception of theory confirmation; hardly any are aware of the rational requirements on theories of any sort.

662.   We live in dark ages: America is the home of born again Christians, a land of Latter Day Saints, of Quakers, Calvinists and Shakers, of Methodists, Lutherans and Moonies, of Hare Krishnas, Presbyterians, Unitarians, Scientologists, Episcopalians and Baptists, Catholics, Jews, Holy Rollers, Christian Scientists, Satanists, Southern Graham Crackers and indefinitely many other cultists and varieties of Hell's Angels.

663.   America's television screens are filled, night and day, with clean shiny pious fat faces, filmed in close, uptight, babbling about Jesus, God and the Devil. There are signs everywhere that Jesus is coming, printed in bold red letters on bumper stickers and billboards. There are tall buildings in New York City with a fourteenth but without a thirteenth floor. Citizens make magical passes in the air when facing crosses or even when a black cat crosses their path. Hostages, freed from the clutches of religious fanatics, humbly thank their father god, and on national television, for their release. America spreads its wings over every form of lunacy, irrationality, one can think of: there is hardly a newspaper without its daily astrological forecast. Millions of people hang mystical symbols, crosses, pentacles, signs of the zodiac, around their craning necks.

664.   Americans make nice distinctions between acts of killing. If a person is killed by an armed robber, we say that he was "murdered"; if the person is killed by the state, we say that he was "executed". The familiar rhetoric, however, should not blind one to the fact that one who is "executed" is killed.

665.   The death penalty is enforced in various states of the United States. In such states, if a person is sentenced to death, he may then be killed by the state on the curious ground that he must "pay for his

crime with his life". What can it possibly mean to say that the person is "paying for his crime with his life"?

666.   That criminals should pay for their crimes by making restitution to their victims makes sense and is intelligible. One who is "executed" makes restitution to no one. If someone "pays for his crime with his life", who receives the payment? Who is being rewarded?

667.   Say that X killed J and then the state killed X. The relatives, friends and associates of J then rejoice: their desire for vengeance, retribution, has been satisfied. The state, by killing X, rewards the vengeful among us.

668.   What if a person, Z, witnesses his friend being murdered, but there is not sufficient evidence to convict the murderer? Z takes it upon himself to kill the murderer. He would then be characterized as a "murderer", or as a "vigilante killer", and would be subject to legal sanctions. Z would generally be deemed to be morally at fault.

669.   There is a difference between a state killing someone and an individual, Z, killing someone. But is there any moral difference between the two acts? In each case, the person killed paid with his life for the crime committed: the desire for vengeance, retribution, was satisfied. However Z, in killing the murderer, became a murderer, whereas a state, in killing X, is not deemed to have murdered X: why not?

670.   There is one obvious legal difference between Z's act of killing to avenge his friend and the state's act of killing to carry out the state's desire for vengeance. Z, in killing the murderer, became himself a murderer, for in killing the murderer he was flouting the law. The state, in contrast, was not flouting the law: one the contrary, the state is legally authorized to kill. "Vengeance is mine, sayeth the State!"

671.   What reason is there to restrict the extraction of vengeance to the state? There is an obvious prudential reason; it may be summed up in a phrase: "crowd control".[69] If anyone could extract vengeance, the

---

[69] I am indebted to Douglas Stalker for this succinct phrase.

result might well be social chaos. Z, in killing to avenge his friend's death, was flouting the law that says that the state, and only the state, may extract vengeance. But that vengeance is the province of the state, and the state alone, is a matter of expedience, not morality: the state has the legal right to kill, but that doesn't mean that it has a moral right to kill. (If we were to consider the killing of X from a prudential, rather than from a moral, point of view, to sentence X to death is economically imprudent: the cost of the permanent incarceration of X is likely to be less than the cost of endless judicial appeals. Do citizens of the state "deserve" to incur this increased expense? One might say "They should pay for their desire for vengeance!")

672.   "Isn't it immoral to flout the law?" That depends on what law and what morality is in question. Not long ago in the South there were laws, or at least *de facto* laws, to the effect that blacks could not sit at the same lunch counters as whites, that blacks could not sit in the front seats of a bus: according to many moralities, there was nothing immoral in flouting such laws. (And anyway, according to my morality, it is absolutely immoral to kill in the pursuit of vengeance, no matter whether the killer be a state or an individual; indeed, all acts of vengeance are immoral.)

673.   Did Z have any warrant to kill the murderer? One could argue that, in killing the murderer, he was protecting the society from further acts of aggression; thus, in the extended sense of "self-defense", he was acting in self-defense. No other alternative was available to him. But, of course, this is a bogus defense: Z killed to avenge the death of his friend.

674.   What warrant, what moral reason, did the state have to kill X? Certainly the state could not sensibly claim to have acted in self-defense! Other alternatives were and are available to the state, the most obvious being the permanent incarceration of X.

675.   (Since death is inevitable for every living thing, X will die, sooner or later: in time the permanent incarceration of X would accomplish the same end as the execution of X. Indeed, if vengeance is what is wanted, then, depending on X's character and sensibility, permanent incarceration might be more severe than immediate

execution[70]: there have, in fact, been persons who demanded immediate execution rather than face a life in prison.)

676.   Neither could the state sensibly appeal to the fact that it was legally authorized to kill X, for that would be to claim that the killing of X was self-warranting. The state was authorized by the state to kill in the pursuit of vengeance: just so, Z was authorized by Z to kill in the pursuit of vengeance.

677.   "But", one might object, "the authority of the state derives from the authority of the citizens of the state. Hence it is the citizens of the state that authorize the killing." If many authorize a killing does that make it less morally objectionable than if only one authorizes the killing? One could just as well argue that, other factors aside, if there are two lynchings, the lynching by the larger mob is less morally objectionable than that by the smaller mob.

678.   For the state to kill someone there must be some individual or group of individuals that act as an agent or as agents of the state: there must be one or more executioners: someone has to pull the switch or release the gas pellet or administer the lethal injection or fire the shot. Let E be an executioner. What warrant does E have to kill X?

679.   Should one excuse E on the grounds that he was only following orders? That is, of course, the excuse given by the Nazis who killed the Jews in German concentration camps. The Nazis in the camps were authorized and ordered by their state to kill: E is authorized and ordered by a state to kill. The Nazis in the camps were murderers: isn't E also a murderer? Indeed, the excuse of the Nazis is better than the suggested excuse for E. If the Nazis in the camps did not follow orders, they might be killed: if E didn't follow orders, he would merely be dismissed.

680.   Can one argue that, in killing X, E is killing someone who "doesn't deserve to live", or one who has "forfeited his right to life"?

---

[70] With respect to the severity of life imprisonment, see John Stuart Mill, "Speech in Favor of Capital Punishment (1868)" in *Punishment*, eds. Joel Feinberg and Hyman Gross (Encino, California: Dickenson Publishing Co., 1975) pp. 121-124.

But the very same argument could be given with respect to Z's killing the person who murdered his friend. If X has "forfeited his right to life", hasn't the person who murdered Z's friend also "forfeited his right to life"? And if Z is a murderer, isn't E also a murderer?

681.   There is no acceptable excuse for E's killing X that is not also an excuse for Z's act of killing. There is no moral reason for the state to authorize, to condone, E and yet to condemn Z.

682.   A morality that condones killing by the state, by agents of the state, thus by certain individuals, in the pursuit of vengeance, but condemns killing by other individuals in their pursuit of vengeance is logically incoherent.[71]

683.   There is, furthermore, a further difficulty with a morality that condones capital punishment: one must consider the symbolic significance of the act of execution.

684.   Previously I said that justice demands and provides affirmation of our moral values: the incarceration of a murderer is a symbolic act in support of our moral values. To incarcerate the murderer may or may not be evil, but not to affirm our moral values would be a greater evil. The moral value being affirmed by the incarceration of the murderer is that it is morally wrong to kill a person.

685.   One must be clear about what moral value is being, and can be, affirmed by the just incarceration of a person.

686.   Consider a person who has captured and imprisoned some innocent person. He, the kidnapper, is then captured by the authorities and sentenced to imprisonment. The moral value being affirmed cannot be that it is wrong to imprison someone: one cannot sensibly affirm a moral value that it is wrong to do x by doing x. The moral value being affirmed is that which is based on the principle that all persons have the right to life, liberty and the pursuit of happiness. It is morally wrong to imprison someone without good and sufficient reason. Hence the moral value being affirmed is not that it is wrong to

---

[71] For a detailed analysis of coherence, see *Epistemic Analysis*, Chapter IV.

do x, but it is wrong to do y, where y is that it is morally wrong to imprison someone without good and sufficient reason. Thus the court is not affirming a moral value that it is wrong to do x by doing x: it is affirming a moral value that it is wrong to do x by invoking y.

687.   What moral value is affirmed in the act of execution that would not be affirmed by the permanent incarceration of the murderer? It could not be that it is morally wrong to kill a person: one could not coherently affirm such a value by killing a person: "Since it is wrong to kill, I will kill you" sayeth the irrational state.

688.   Say that the moral value being affirmed is that it is wrong to kill a person without good and sufficient reason. But what possible good and sufficient reason could the state have to execute, to kill, someone? Neither self-defense nor self-preservation could be relevant considerations since the state has the option of permanent incarceration.

689.   Some might say "Justice demands a balance: consider the scales in the archetypal image of Justice. The scales are not balanced, in the case of a heinous murderer, simply by the permanent incarceration of the murderer: more is required and that more is supplied by the death penalty, by capital punishment."

690.   But how does the execution of the murderer serve to balance the scales of justice? The execution of the murderer might serve to affirm the doctrine of "An eye for an eye, a tooth for a tooth", but that would not be an affirmation of any moral value. The same can be said for "As ye sow, so shall ye reap", etc. These are doctrines, not moral values.

691.   Say the murderer is a serial killer: he has killed many people. (Isn't E, the executioner, and the state, also a serial killer?) Doesn't the act of execution implicate the judgment that the life that is taken is essentially and necessarily without any value?

692.   Such a judgment would simply be mistaken. When there are executions, e.g., in Raleigh, North Carolina, there are almost invariably two groups outside the prison where the execution is to take place. One, a group that is rejoicing, the other, a group that is

mourning. The latter is likely to include the family and friends of the person to be executed: his or her life is of value to them. There are, furthermore, persons to whom any and every life is of some value.

693.   Isn't the symbolic act of execution an affirmation of the valuelessness of the life that is taken? Such an affirmation, however, would not be an affirmation of any moral value.

694.   The only moral value that could possibly be in question is that it is wrong to kill without good and sufficient reason. That cannot be affirmed by killing a person without good and sufficient reason.

695.   Symbolism and imagery constitute the real and only basis of the moralities that I have endeavored to characterize here, my own morality and that of others. But the most fundamental image of all of my morality is that which is created by an appreciation of life, all life.

696.   Life is not a god-given miracle: every living entity is a finite organic automaton constituted by a fortuitous combination of particles. Unlike mechanical automata, living entities are subject to growth and maturation, and, as everything else, living beings are subject to inevitable entropic degradation. The fate of Humpty Dumpty awaits us all. But, while perched on our wall, there is much to see, to hear, to taste and, above all, to understand and appreciate before we fall.

697.   I am using the word 'appreciate' in its primary sense: that sense in which one speaks of appreciating a position in chess, or in which one can say 'I appreciate what you have done: I mean to make you pay for it'. It has nothing to do with liking, or being grateful and the like. It is a matter of sizing up whatever is in question, of perceiving and attending to its various features and the interrelationships between its various features. *Homo Sapiens* has the absolutely marvelous capacity to appreciate this world (which is not to suggest that this capacity is generally exercised).

698.   The number of living entities on earth is unknown and unknowable. In my small garden alone, there are probably over a million living things growing and reproducing: earthworms, without whose labor we should have no top soil, beautiful weeds, which is to say, beautiful herbaceous vegetation that is generally unwanted.

(Weeds are to grass what noise is to sound.) There are arachnids and ants and small toads, birds and bees and tall trees. If one is to appreciate life, one must see such a garden as it is: teeming with life.

699.　Not all of it is friendly to man or woman. There are black widows and brown recluses. There are copperheads. Here and there, there may be some poison ivy or poison oak. Foraging ants may invade one's house: termites may bring it crashing down. There are yellow jackets (family *Vespidae*), social wasps that commonly nest in the ground, that invariably make me flee for fear of being stung, being as I am, intensely allergic to their venom.

700.　I put down chemical barriers to prevent the ants and termites from entering my house. And as for the yellow jackets, of course I could kill them: there are pesticides available for just that purpose. But why should I do that? It's easy enough to avoid them. If one enters my house, I do my best to capture it and then release it outside. The same is true for black widows and brown recluses: they are simply evicted, unharmed. Copperheads avoid me as I avoid them: we each go our own way.

701.　It's easy to kill but then, it is impossible to undo what one has done: "Not all the King's horses and all the King's men." Before the inevitable fall, what can one do but enjoy it all?

702.　If I had the skill of Andrew Marvell, which I do not, perhaps then I could evoke the image of life that is wanted here.

What wondrous Life in this I lead!
Ripe Apples drop about my head;
The Luscious Clusters of the Vine
Upon my Mouth do crush their Wine;
The Nectaren, and curious Peach,
Into my hands themselves do reach;
Stumbling on Melons, as I pass,
Insnar'd with Flow'rs, I fall on Grass.[72]

---

[72] Andrew Marvell, from *The Garden*

703.   Unfortunately, most of us do not live in Marvell's marvelous garden: most of the people in this world are forced to face the bitter necessities of life. All too many live "in rats' alley Where the dead men lost their bones".[73] They stumble, ensnared, not with flowers, but by trash; they fall on feces, not on grass.

704.   But we are not here concerned with an appreciation of the lives that people lead: we are concerned with an appreciation of life itself. That many persons lead miserable lives in no way denigrates the value of life.

705.   The only life we know is that here on Earth. It seems most likely that there is life elsewhere in the universe, but, as yet, we do not know that. We do know that life here on Earth is incredibly rich and varied. The amazing arachnids rival *Homo Sapiens* in the variety of their habitats: they are to be found high up on Everest and in the depths of the Amazon. Perhaps somewhere in the Everglades, at high noon on any sunny day, there is an alligator (*Alligator mississipiensis*) lying on a mud bank, basking in the hot sun.[74] Seen from the side, the gator appears to have a great healthy grin conveying a sense of well being, of vitality and life.

---

[73] From T. S. Eliot's *The Waste Land*, II A GAME OF CHESS.

[74] See Paul Ziff, *Antiaesthetics* (Dordrecht, Holland: D. Reidel Pub. Co., 1984) VIII "Anything Viewed".

INDEX

PHILOSOPHICAL STUDIES SERIES

PHILOSOPHICAL STUDIES SERIES

PHILOSOPHICAL STUDIES SERIES

52. Jesús Ezquerro and Jesús M. Larrazabal (eds.): *Cognition, Semantics and Philosophy*. Proceedings of the First International Colloquium on Cognitive Science. 1992   ISBN 0-7923-1538-3

53. O.H. Green: *The Emotions*. A Philosophical Theory. 1992   ISBN 0-7923-1549-9

54. Jeffrie G. Murphy: *Retribution Reconsidered*. More Essays in the Philosophy of Law. 1992
    ISBN 0-7923-1815-3

55. Phillip Montague: *In the Interests of Others*. An Essay in Moral Philosophy. 1992
    ISBN 0-7923-1856-0

56. Jacques-Paul Dubucs (ed.): *Philosophy of Probability*. 1993   ISBN 0-7923-2385-8

57. Gary S. Rosenkrantz: *Haecceity*. An Ontological Essay. 1993   ISBN 0-7923-2438-2

58. Charles Landesman: *The Eye and the Mind*. Reflections on Perception and the Problem of
    Knowledge. 1994   ISBN 0-7923-2586-9

59. Paul Weingartner (ed.): *Scientific and Religious Belief*. 1994   ISBN 0-7923-2595-8

60. Michaelis Michael and John O'Leary-Hawthorne (eds.): *Philosophy in Mind*. The Place of
    Philosophy in the Study of Mind. 1994   ISBN 0-7923-3143-5

61. William H. Shaw: *Moore on Right and Wrong*. The Normative Ethics of G.E. Moore. 1995
    ISBN 0-7923-3223-7

62. T.A. Blackson: *Inquiry, Forms, and Substances*. A Study in Plato's Metaphysics and Epistem-
    ology. 1995   ISBN 0-7923-3275-X

63. Debra Nails: *Agora, Academy, and the Conduct of Philosophy*. 1995   ISBN 0-7923-3543-0

64. Warren Shibles: *Emotion in Aesthetics*. 1995   ISBN 0-7923-3618-6

65. John Biro and Petr Kotatko (eds.): *Frege: Sense and Reference One Hundred Years Later*. 1995
    ISBN 0-7923-3795-6

66. Mary Gore Forrester: *Persons, Animals, and Fetuses*. An Essay in Practical Ethics. 1996
    ISBN 0-7923-3918-5

67. K. Lehrer, B.J. Lum, B.A. Slichta and N.D. Smith (eds.): *Knowledge, Teaching and Wisdom*.
    1996   ISBN 0-7923-3980-0

68. Herbert Granger: *Aristotle's Idea of the Soul*. 1996   ISBN 0-7923-4033-7

69. Andy Clark, Jesús Ezquerro and Jesús M. Larrazabal (eds.): *Philosophy and Cognitive Sci-
    ence: Categories, Consciousness, and Reasoning*. Proceedings of the Second International
    Colloquium on Cogitive Science. 1996   ISBN 0-7923-4068-X

70. J. Mendola: *Human Thought*. 1997   ISBN 0-7923-4401-4

71. J. Wright: *Realism and Explanatory Priority*. 1997   ISBN 0-7923-4484-7

72. X. Arrazola, K. Korta and F.J. Pelletier (eds.): *Discourse, Interaction and Communication*.
    Proceedings of the Fourth International Colloquium on Cognitive Science. 1998
    ISBN 0-7923-4952-0

73. E. Morscher, O. Neumaier and P. Simons (eds.): *Applied Ethics in a Troubled World*. 1998
    ISBN 0-7923-4965-2

74. R.O. Savage: *Real Alternatives, Leibniz's Metaphysics of Choice*. 1998 ISBN 0-7923-5057-X

75. Q. Gibson: *The Existence Principle*. 1998   ISBN 0-7923-5188-6

76. F. Orilia and W.J. Rapaport (eds.): *Thought, Language, and Ontology*. 1998
    ISBN 0-7923-5197-5

PHILOSOPHICAL STUDIES SERIES

77. J. Bransen and S.E. Cuypers (eds.): *Human Action, Deliberation and Causation.* 1998
                                                            ISBN 0-7923-5204-1
78. R.D. Gallie: *Thomas Reid: Ethics, Aesthetics and the Anatomy of the Self.* 1998
                                                            ISBN 0-7923-5241-6
79. K. Korta, E. Sosa and X. Arrazola (eds.): *Cognition, Agency and Rationality.* Proceedings of
     the Fifth International Colloquium on Cognitive Science. 1999   ISBN 0-7923-5973-9
80. M. Paul: *Success in Referential Communication.* 1999   ISBN 0-7923-5974-7
81. E. Fischer: *Linguistic Creativity.* Exercises in 'Philosophical Therapy'. 2000
                                                            ISBN 0-7923-6124-5
82. R. Tuomela: *Cooperation.* A Philosophical Study. 2000   ISBN 0-7923-6201-2
83. P. Engel (ed.): *Believing and Accepting.* 2000   ISBN 0-7923-6238-1
84. W.L. Craig: *Time and the Metaphysics of Relativity.* 2000   ISBN 0-7923-6668-9
85. D.A. Habibi: *John Stuart Mill and the Ethic of Human Growth.* 2001
                                                            ISBN 0-7923-6854-1
86. M. Slors: *The Diachronic Mind.* An Essay on Personal Identity, Psychological Continuity and
     the Mind-Body Problem. 2001   ISBN 0-7923-6978-5
87. L.N. Oaklander (ed.): *The Importance of Time.* Proceedings of the Philosophy of Time Society,
     1995–2000. 2001   ISBN 1-4020-0062-6
88. M. Watkins: *Rediscovering Colors.* A Study in Pollyanna Realism. 2002
                                                            ISBN 1-4020-0737-X
89. W.F. Vallicella: *A Paradigm Theory of Existence.* Onto–Theology Vindicated. 2002
                                                            ISBN 1-4020-0887-2
90. M. Hulswit: *From Cause to Causation.* A Peircean Perspective. 2002
                                            ISBN 1-4020-0976-3; Pb 1-4020-0977-1
91. D. Jacquette (ed.): *Philosophy, Psychology, and Psychologism.* Critical and Historical Readings
     on the Psychological Turn in Philosophy. 2003   ISBN 1-4020-1337-X
92. G. Preyer, G. Peter and M. Ulkan (eds.): *Concepts of Meaning.* Framing an Integrated Theory
     of Linguistic Behavior. 2003   ISBN 1-4020-1329-9
93. W. de Muijnck: *Dependencies, Connections, and Other Relations.* A Theory of Mental Caus-
     ation. 2003   ISBN 1-4020-1391-4
94. N. Milkov: *A Hundred Years of English Philosophy.* 2003   ISBN 1-4020-1432-5
95. E.J. Olsson (ed.): *The Epistomology of Keith Lehrer.* 2003   ISBN 1-4020-1605-0
96. D.S. Clarke: *Sign Levels.* Language and Its Evolutionary Antecedents. 2003
                                                            ISBN 1-4020-1650-6
97. A. Meirav: *Wholes, Sums and Unities.* 2003   ISBN 1-4020-1660-3
98. C.H. Conn: *Locke on Esence and Identity.* 2003   ISBN 1-4020-1670-0
99. J.M. Larrazabal and L.A. Pérez Miranda: *Language, Knowledge, and Representation.* Pro-
     ceedings of the Sixth International Colloquium on Cognitive Science (LCC-99). 2004
                                                            ISBN 1-4020-2057-0
100. P. Ziff: *Moralities.* A Diachronic Evolution Approach. 2004   ISBN 1-4020-1891-6
101. J.A. Corlett: Terorism: *A Philosophical Analysis.* 2003
                                            ISBN 1-4020-1694-8; Pb 1-4020-1695-6

PHILOSOPHICAL STUDIES SERIES

KLUWER ACADEMIC PUBLISHERS – DORDRECHT / BOSTON / LONDON

Printed in Great Britain
by Amazon

78318933R00106